The Homemaker's Favorite Helper

Heloise is the syndicated newspaper columnist whose original, light-hearted approach to housework has won her a following of millions of women readers.

Here Heloise provides hundreds of new hints and how-to's for everything, *all around the house*.

Arranged alphabetically, this book also has a quick index—for finding the answer to your problem when you need the answer most!

Save money, save time, save energy—call for tips from Heloise.

Heloise All Around the House
was originally published by
Prentice-Hall, Inc.

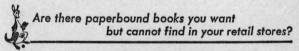

Heloise
ALL AROUND
THE HOUSE

by

Heloise

❦

ILLUSTRATED

PUBLISHED BY POCKET BOOKS NEW YORK

HELOISE ALL AROUND THE HOUSE

Prentice-Hall edition published July, 1965

POCKET BOOK edition published March, 1967

11th printing........August, 1972

This POCKET BOOK edition includes every word
contained in the original, higher-priced edition. It is printed
from brand-new plates made from completely reset, clear, easy-to-read
type. POCKET BOOK editions are published by POCKET BOOKS, a division
of Simon & Schuster, Inc., 630 Fifth Avenue, New York, N.Y. 10020.
Trademarks registered in the United States and other countries.

L

With all my heart and devotion, I dedicate this book to my homemakers . . . the precious backbone of the world.

Contents

prologue

a

b

c

page 34

d

page 51

e

page 62

f

page 66

g

page 71

j

page 95

Many a Jewel of an Idea Here

k

page 97

Let That Kitchen Clutter Go, Go, Go! • Get Out Hidden Dirt • Simple as A, B, C • Tend to Your Knitting!

l

page 101

Taking the Ugh! Out of Laundry Day • Let the Drip-Dries Save You Work • Wash Those Good Dresses by Hand • Getting the Hang of It • Cut Laundry Costs • Curtains for the Birds • No Slip While They Drip • Maybe Your Machine's Just Thirsty • Cut Down On Your Soaking • Rust-Proof Your Washing • White on White • Try This • Spray Treatment for Jeans • Roll Away Creases • Salt Boxes Keep Laundry Room Tidy • Secrets of the Not-So-Inscrutable Orient • New Life for Old Lamp Shades • Better Leather Longer • Caution is the Word in Linen Storage

m

page 117

n

page 128

o

page 132

p

page 134

q

page 146

r

page 148

s

page 158

t

page 189

u

page 195

v

page 196

Instant Upholstery Job • The Velvet Touch • Beating an Old Bugaboo—Venetian Blinds • There's That Vinegar Again! • Vinegar Rinse for Socks

w

page 200

Ways with Walls • When You Change Brands • Try Salt-Water Treatment • No More Tangles • Sockeroo of an Idea! • Roll-on Wax • Wedding White • Watch Those Windows • Jack Frost Was Here! • Windshield Tricks • ". . . Have You Any Wool?"

x

page 207

X-tra, X-tra, Read All About It! • Leg Art • Happiness Is a Plastic Jug • Two Ideas from New Zealand • Cracker-Barrel Philosophy • Hot Lunch • A Bachelor Speaks • Be Prepared • Does Everything but the Dishes . . . • Did You Ever Think of . . . ? • Odds and Ends That Work! • Timely Tips • Storm Signals • Feeling Clothesed In? • Dowel the Towels • Tip from Sir Galahad • Quick Tricks

y
page 215

z
page 218

epilogue
page 219

index
page 223

Prologue

Being a housewife is not a fault . . . it's a glory. And I want every woman, mother and homemaker to know that I think we have the greatest job in the whole wide world.

I would like all of you homemakers, business women, and bachelor girls to tag along with me from room to room in our homes and discover hundreds of marvelous shortcuts. I hope these hints will make housekeeping less time-consuming and more fun.

Let's tackle the problems with gusto, but let our daily moods (rather than the day of the week) dictate which task to do at a given time. Who says you have to wash on Monday, iron on Tuesday, deep-clean on Wednesday . . . etc., etc?

Your Sabbath is the *only* day of the week which should be set aside for specific things . . . thanks-giving, rest, and so forth.

If you do your little chores while you are in the mood, you will do them much faster, more thoroughly, and you will expend less energy.

Even though we all like a clean, orderly home because it brings pleasure and peace of mind, we must remember that no housewife has ever had her home in *perfect* order. So don't try to make or keep yours that way. It's a lost cause. And the world will still go 'round. Remember, Rome wasn't built in a day—and it still isn't finished!

Don't knock yourself out worrying about where to start first. Try to learn to top-clean first. Just make your bed, put the breakfast dishes to soak, and pick up the big pieces. Then go back and get the little things done along with the deep cleaning. Once the top looks nice it lends peace of mind, and that is what we work for all our lives.

If you feel in the mood to give the kitchen a thorough cleaning, drop everything else and clean it. Wow . . . !

If you feel like rearranging the living room, hop to it! Then sit down and have a cup of coffee while you admire the results.

Take pride in making your bed, washing your dishes, laundering your husband's and children's clothing, preparing a meal, cleaning Venetian blinds, sweeping the floor. . . .

A housewife needs so much courage to face the ordinary daily tasks of running a home. There are days when we all feel gloomy and sometimes the tiniest chore is a huge burden. But *pick up that courage,* gals, and say to yourself "Life is grand"—whether you are washing the dishes or cooking dinner.

Let's make homemaking an exciting adventure, rather than drudgery. And let's learn to find satisfaction in a job done to the best of our abilities and energies.

Enjoy life, and you'll enjoy housekeeping more. It can be fun, if you learn to "live a little" while you're doing it.

And, don't forget gals . . . the *second* wife usually has the maid!

Each chapter of this book was written just for you, and was made possible because of you and all my wonderful readers.

Heloise

Heloise
All Around
The House

a

FIRST, PRECAUTION, SECOND, AID

Have you ever seen a stunned mother and father standing outside the emergency room door in a hospital waiting . . . waiting . . . and the father saying, "That's my baby girl," as the tears rolled down his cheeks?

For this child it was too late. The child had swallowed poison and some poisons have no antidote! If you just knew what was under your sink and in your cabinets that could cause this same scene (it might not be your own child, but could be the child from next door), you would scurry immediately and put these things out of the reach of young ones and the oldsters who can't see clearly.

Yes . . . even those sleeping pills and aspirin tablets and tranquilizers on your bedside table! They are dynamite . . . not to you, perhaps, but to someone else. Other poisons are like coiled snakes in your cabinets.

Most **accidents** occur in the safest place . . . home!

Look at your cabinets . . . under your sink . . . on your bedside table . . . around your washing machine. . . .

Store all medicines, cleaning and polishing agents out of the reach of children.

Never call medicine "candy." Frankly tell a child that you are taking medicine when he sees you doing so.

Seventeen million youngsters in the United States alone are injured or killed each year. Over 90 percent of these accidents would not have happened if precautions had been taken. This figure may be almost completely eliminated if you, my dear friend, will help.

Hide all that aspirin (twelve adult aspirins could kill a child, know that?), sleeping pills, pep pills, furniture polish, kerosene, ammonia, cleaning compounds, bleach and insecticides.

Eliminate burns, which are mostly caused when mothers neglect to turn the handle of a pot or pan around, backward or sideways, when something is cooking on the stove. Be sure that a child cannot reach and grab for that pot or pan! When he smells good food, he's curious.

If an accident does happen, emergency treatment is most important.

Are you aware that household ammonia in an eye (sometimes we drop a bottle or it splashes when poured) can cause blindness unless first aid is given *immediately?* If ammonia splashes in an eye, lay the child down on the drainboard and hold his head under a gentle spray and wash out the eye for at least ten minutes. If it happens to an adult, bathe his eye under the faucet, or make him lie down and literally pour water over his eye—lots of water. Or put him under the shower to wash out the eye thoroughly. Call your doctor, hospital emergency room, police or fire department. Those firemen are equipped for nearly anything!

Next, if you are on the verge of hysterics, dial "O" for operator on your phone. She is the best friend we have when we have difficulty making sense. And when you get on the phone, don't forget these two very important things:

State your address first! (Just in case you collapse—and it happens often.) Then state what's happened so far so she can call the proper place and get help to you in a hurry. She knows.

Don't hang up the phone! Leave it off the hook so the operator can hear you. She wants to know what's going on so she can call more help if needed.

If you go to a hospital, remember (if possible) to take with you the bottle of whatever-it-was that Johnnie drank. The doctor will need that label. There are thousands of products on the market today and the hospital should have the bottle in order to know what to use as an antidote. If they do not have the answer, your doctor will telephone the manufacturer and find out what it takes to save your child's life.

Let me impress upon you . . . *Don't* put your child in the car and rush him to the hospital without first calling a hospital or doctor. The first five minutes may mean the difference between life and death. Life is precious. You can't buy it, trade it, or redeem it! All you can do is try to save it.

For those who have poor eyesight or have children in the house, one way to avoid swallowing poison or using poisonous items by mistake is to take a strip of sandpaper and tape it around the bottle with the sanding side out. That way, if you pick up the bottle you will immediately notice the rough surface and look twice at the contents.

Another thing to do if you have bad eyesight is to tie a little bell around the neck of any bottle. Immediately, you will notice if you have taken something poisonous from the shelf.

Don't ever mix straight household bleach with vinegar to clean *anything*. It produces a poisonous gas. Boils like a volcano! Bad.

Some types of toilet cleaners should not have bleaches mixed with them, either. The mixture also produces poisonous fumes.

If your toilet bowl cleaner doesn't do the job, try another brand. But never mix anything with it. No need to die over a toilet bowl that needs cleaning. Be careful of mixing chemicals. It's a dangerous job for the chemist . . . let alone for you.

CALL AN EXPERT

When someone has fallen and you suspect a broken bone, don't move him! Call for expert help . . . a doctor, the police, an ambulance or your local fire department.

Shock is another thing to be careful about after an accident. Help prevent it by covering the injured person with a blanket, coat or any clothing you happen to have around. Warmth is most necessary for injured persons.

If a child falls, don't always consider it a bump! Watch him. If he gets drowsy, vomits or bleeds from the mouth, nose or ears, or just wants to sleep, or if he gets numb anywhere . . . call your doctor! Don't give him *anything* to eat or drink *until* you have talked with a doctor.

DANGER IS YOUR BUSINESS

Watch your electrical cords and outlets. These are dangerous. For your own safety, don't have a frayed or damaged electrical cord around the house.

Don't keep any electrical gadgets, such as radios or TV sets (yes, many people take along portable TV's) in the bathroom! Don't try to shave with a electric razor while taking a bath! This can electrocute people . . . that's you, my dear!

ICE TO THE RESCUE

When a child gets a splinter in his hand or finger, hold an ice cube on the splinter for a few minutes before removing it. This numbs the area and you will be surprised how painless removing a splinter becomes.

If a young child hurts his lip and refuses to put ice on it, let him eat a popsicle . . . the swelling will be gone by the time the popsicle is finished.

PROTECT YOUR CHILDREN FROM SHOCK

From a safety-minded mother: "I think every mother of small babies who crawl should know not to leave a socket in the wall unprotected. This means that there should be a plug in the socket itself or that the socket should be protected from the baby.

"A piece of cellophane tape or adhesive tape or even a Band-Aid can be applied in a minute over the two little holes, thus preventing shock should the baby pick up a hairpin or bobby pin and try to stick it in the socket."

TAKING THE TICK OUT OF THE TOCK

If the ticking of an **alarm clock** keeps you awake, set it on the floor on top of a thick throw rug or a soft pillow and the noise will be cut down tremendously—yet the clock will be where you can reach out and turn it off without having to get out of bed.

For those who have acute hearing and cannot stand the loud bell of an alarm clock . . . did you know that you can take a plain old rubber band and place it around the bell?

All you have to do is open the back of the clock and look for the alarm.

The thicker the rubber band, the quieter the alarm!

If you are a deep sleeper and your **alarm clock** fails to wake you up, set it on a pie tin!

CAUSE FOR ALARM!

From Johnnie's mother: "My little boy just cannot learn time. He is five years old. He has been late for dinner sometimes ten nights in a row.

"We finally decided that we could tie an **alarm clock** on the bottom of his tricycle (under the seat) and set it for 5:30 P.M. No matter where he is, when the clock goes off, either he or some of his friends will hear it and he scoots home real quick. Works like a charm. Now I even use this method at noon! He loves it."

LET AMMONIA DO THE DIRTY WORK!

A young bride asks: "How does one remove the brown from the outside of hammered aluminum pans?"

Except for plain old ordinary elbow grease, broken fingernails, and a soap-filled scouring pad . . . the only answer I know is **ammonia.**

I have a friend who had a hammered aluminum skillet that was thirty years old and had *never* been cleaned on the outside.

I turned the pan upside down, placed an old piece of terry cloth bath towel over the skillet, poured about half a cup of ammonia on it, and immediately placed it in a plastic bag and tied the loose ends with a rubber band.

I let this sit overnight.

The next morning I took a soap-filled pad and scrubbed the bottom of this thirty-year-old skillet. I couldn't believe it . . . the layers and layers of carbon immediately started coming off! The skillet was shining within five minutes! My friend was as shocked as I.

If your pot has years of *accumulated* carbon, don't think you can do this in one operation. Because, remember . . . if it took years to get *all those layers* of carbon on, you're not about to get if off in five minutes. It may take two operations, even if I did manage to do my friend's in one.

I want to let you know that the directions on the ammonia bottle say, "Do not use ammonia on aluminum. It pits." However, when a pan is thirty years old . . . who cares as long as it gets clean?

My friend was delighted with her skillet. She saw no pits and neither did I.

The plastic bag keeps the fumes of the ammonia from completely gassing *you!* Also, from the research I have done, I feel that the fumes of the ammonia do the dirty work for you, rather than the liquid.

GET SET FOR THE SETTING

Make a "hair-do" **apron** from a large bath towel that has become too thin for good drying. Fold in half crosswise, cut out a circle to fit the neck and cut an opening down the front. Bind with bias tape. This also helps use up odds and ends of tape!

Sew a large pocket at the bottom of the apron. It can be made from a washcloth or from the circular piece cut from the neck hole. Make a smaller narrow pocket on the other side.

In the large pocket keep rollers or clips. In the small pocket keep your comb. This is easy to work with when putting your hair up, keeps your dress clean, and is easy to launder as it needs no ironing.

I put this hair-do apron on when I take my hair down. I put the curlers in the large pocket, the comb in the narrow pocket and put the apron away. By doing this, everything is ready when I want to "do up" my hair the next time.

FOR GOOD MEASURE!

From Utah: "For those who can never find their measuring tape, make yourself a sewing **apron!**

"I find this one of the most useful things in my home. Just sew a measuring tape upside down across the bottom of the apron. . . . This is for good measure!

"It's handy when you are sitting at your sewing machine. You can just lift the bottom edge of your apron and check the width of any seam or hem you happen to be stitching.

"These aprons sell well at church bazaars."

FOR THE BUDDING ARTIST

Here's a fingerpaint recipe for the young **artist of the** family. It's wonderful for mothers who have to make their own paints.

Mix one cup of corn starch (or laundry starch) with enough cold water to make a smooth, thin paste. Add one cup of flaked soap chips and one-half cup of salt.

Put this mixture in a double boiler and add one quart of water and cook until it's thick. Increase amount of water if necessary.

Beat it with an egg beater, put it into empty baby food jars and put some food coloring in each jar.

One teaspoon of glycerine makes this more pliable and easier on the hands. The salt acts as a preservative.

A harmless paint for the kiddies to play with is made by simply adding food coloring to some canned milk!

Here are some more fingerpainting hints from other mothers:

Broken rolls of wallpaper can be bought for a "song." These are great for little kiddies to paint on. Use the backside of the wallpaper for fingerpainting.

Some mothers add vanilla to the paint. Yep, the kind we use in cooking. Smells good.

Many teachers have written that they add a few drops of oil of cloves to the mixture.

Suggestion: Put newspapers down on a table before a child starts painting on anything! Sure saves lots of wear on the nerves and cleaning up messes later.

CAR-WASHING MADE EASY

Do you hate to wash your **automobile?**

Don't worry, we all do!

But I have found an easy way that is really a quickie and also completely satisfactory, according to the hundreds of responses I have gotten on it.

Ever tried washing that automobile with a bucket of water and about a cup of kerosene? Yes, just a cup of plain old kerosene poured into a plastic bucket, which should hold at least one gallon of warm water.

Dip a sponge (not the kitchen sponge, as it probably contains grease and oils from kitchen wiping) or a piece of clean terry cloth in the mixture and squeeze it out slightly.

Start at the top of the car, and using a circular motion, go over the entire car. Then take a clean old bath towel and just gently wipe the car from top to bottom. That's all there is to it.

This method has many good points beside saving energy. Not only can I wash our car in half the time, but it has relieved our family of waxing. I have used this method on our car for nearly three years and we have not waxed it in all that time.

The best part of it is that no mater how dirty your car is, it will not need wetting down beforehand. This method removes soil, dirt and splashes at the same time. If your car is very big or extra dirty, it may take a change of water and kerosene mixture, but this is unlikely.

When it rains the car will actually bead water! Try spot-testing it yourself. Wash a fender, as a sample, then hose it.

When used on chrome, this method is fantastic. Many persons have told me that it has prevented rust.

Use no wax with this method. It will *not* work on cars that have become oxidized. The oxidization must first be removed with a cleaner.

If you have small rust spots on your bumper try this: briskly "scrub" the rust spots with a piece of foil which has been crumpled up. I have had many letters from electroplating companies saying this works wonders.

Do not hose the car down before or afterward. No need to.

The car can be washed in half the time it ordinarily takes with a garden hose, and doesn't make a mess of water in your driveway, either.

This is an especially good method if you live in an apartment house and have no access to a water hose, or if you have a landlord who won't let you use his hose. (I have been in that spot, too.) Take your bucket of warm water to the park and drive it up under a big shady tree and enjoy the day.

The only complaint I have had in three years was from a car-wash man who said that I had ruined his business!

From Virginia: "Here is an idea for short women who have to wash their own **automobile.** I am less than five feet and I wash the top of the car with my string mop! (No matter how many boxes I stand on, I still cannot reach the top center of the car without the mop.)

"The long handle helps in reaching across the top and sides without stretching or stooping or getting so close to the car that I get all wet!

"The string mop does not scratch the car, and has saved me many falls."

A SHADE OF DIFFERENCE

From Maryland: "I always keep a discarded window shade in the trunk of my **auto.** Then if I have to get out and change a tire or have any kind of trouble, I unroll the shade on the ground; it helps keep my clothes clean while I work on the car."

STARTING FROM SCRATCH!

From Detroit: "Here's a money-saving idea for the family **automobile,** as well as a nifty trick.

"One time there was a scratch on our car. I took a matching color crayon and worked it into the scratch itself. I found that you can hardly see the scratch. You can buff the repaired place with a soft cloth. And the wax in the crayon prevents rusting!"

YOU'LL BE PENNIES AHEAD

From New Jersey: "We always keep from five to ten pennies and a few nickels in the glove compartment of our **automobile.** It's very handy when you don't have the correct pocket change for the parking meters!"

DON'T THROW IN THE TOWEL!

What do you do when the selvage on a **bath towel** becomes ragged?

You will notice on some bath towels that one side has the selvage turned back, and on some others both sides are turned back and stitched by machine. Some bath towels have plain selvages on both sides with no stitching.

After my bath towels are a few years old, and before the selvage wears out completely, I fold the selvage itself back one-fourth of an inch and stitch it twice on my sewing machine. This makes the towel last much longer.

If the selvages become ragged you can take the scissors and cut off that little selvage, then fold the towel back and stitch it with two rows of stitching on your sewing machine.

I find it best to use a *large* stitch when doing this type of work. I also use *mercerized* thread for this job.

If your bath towels become extremely ragged, try cutting them into thirds and hemming all four sides with a double-stitched hem. These make excellent kitchen towels. Far easier for Mother and little kiddies than the usual white kitchen towels. And just what child or husband doesn't pick up your nice clean tea towel to wipe his hands?

BATHING BEAUTIES

From Florida: "A helpful hint that I have for every homemaker is to keep a little rubber hose on her **bathtub** spigot. This is wonderful for washing children's hair, plus your own.

"When I clean the tile and scour the tub I can just turn on the little hose and everything is completely rinsed. In warm weather, the hose is very handy for just soaking and rinsing children to cool them off. A mother can do this several times a day and it takes less time than giving an ordinary bath."

From North Carolina: "One of the hardest parts of **bathing** my one-year-old child was washing her hair without getting shampoo on everything. Now it's easy! I bought a big sponge. Before I start her bath, I pour the shampoo on the sponge. Then it is a simple matter to rub the sponge on her hair. There is no shampoo running in her eyes and no chance of dropping a slippery bottle in the tub."

From Los Angeles: "If mothers would give babies their vitamins while giving them *their* **bath,** there would never be a vitamin stain on their little undershirts! If the baby spits up or dribbles while he bathes, then the mother can wash it off with soap and water while he is in his tub.

"I am wondering how many others know that the skin is so much easier to wash than trying to get the stains out of a T-shirt?"

From Wisconsin: "This may be of interest to mothers who have small children. I keep the soft plastic and rubber animal toys clean (for little mouths) by popping two or three of them into the **bathtub** with my kids each night!

"I just rinse the toys under the hot water and let them dry. Every night I take different toys so they can all be kept clean. It works like a charm!"

From New Mexico: "My two young sons dearly love a long play period in the tub while taking their **baths.** The problem of where to put their many toys, floating boats, etc., was solved when I loaded everything into a heavy plastic bag with holes in it and hung this on the shower nozzle with one of those plastic clothespins with a hook. This lets the bag drip dry, and it may remain until the next evening bathtime. If your heavy plastic bag does not have holes in the bottom . . . make some."

From Virginia: "When the very small fry scream about being lifted out of the **bathtub** (when they want to continue to splash about), simply pull out the plug while the little dears are still in the tub! Oddly enough, when all the water is gone, they don't mind that the fun is all over and will leave to be dried willingly."

From Chicago: "Please do not laugh! I think my suggestion is wonderful for mothers who have small babies past the bathinette stage, but too young for a tub bath.

"I use my plastic clothes **basket to bathe** my baby in when I take my bath in the tub. This basket has holes in it so the water can enter.

"When I draw my tub and take my own bath, I put the clothes basket in the tub of water with me. Then I undress my baby, put him in the clothes basket and get into the tub. This way I have the pleasure of teaching him to pat the water like Mother does . . . to bathe himself, of showing him how to take the washrag to soap his tummy, and of getting him over his fear of water.

"The water swishes through the basket and he absolutely loves it.

"When the bath is over, all I do is pull the plug. Baby stays in his own precious domain while I dry and clothe myself. There is no chance of baby falling on the slippery tub or being in too much water, which might frighten him."

SAVE IT FOR THE CLAMS

To prevent steam from forming in the **bathroom,** run cold water in the tub before putting in the hot water.

WHEN YOU'RE ON THE MAT

Safety hint: When using water softeners, bath salts or oils in your **bath** . . . be *very* careful not to add too much—especially if you do not have a mat in the bottom of your tub. When you stand up in the tub before all the water drains out, the tub may be so slippery that you can fall and injure yourself.

From Idaho: "Not until my husband slipped in the **bathtub** while standing on a rubber mat did I realize that a mat does not remain safe or skidproof without help.

"Once a week, when I give the tub a thorough cleansing, I turn the mat over in the bottom of the tub and sprinkle cleanser on it, too. Then I scrub off the film that accumulates on the mat in spite of the washing it gets after each use. Now the mat sticks to the tub and is safe to stand on during showers."

One woman wrote that the way to keep **bathroom** floor mats and throw rugs from slipping was to put a piece of plastic bag under them! The kind that comes on garments from the dry cleaners.

I couldn't see this for mud. The more I thought about it, the more absurd it seemed. But I tried it. By golly, it works!

My rubber-backed throw rug and my bath mat have practically *stuck* to the floor for three days. They don't wrinkle or slide! My bathroom floor is asphalt, but I don't see why it wouldn't work on anything else. It costs you nothing to try it on your type floor.

From Virginia: "We put our **bath** mats and rubber sink mats right into our automatic washing machine, add a few bath towels, and everything comes out sweet and clean.

"We are owners of a spanking new 40-unit motel and are 100 percent sanitary. A big time-saver is mixing the bath towels with the mats, and we have found it does not hurt the life of the mats."

The roughness of the towels rubs against the rubber mats and scours away the soil. This same principle is applied when a shower curtain is put in a washing machine with two bath towels.

BATHROOM BITS

From Baltimore: "I have found that if I keep a clothespin in the **bathroom** pinned to my shower curtain, I can hang up my shower cap by the point of the head . . . bless pointed heads on women!

"For years I put my shower cap on a hook on the wall only to find that it gathered moisture and mildew around the band. This method—using a clothespin to hang it up—allows all the water and moisture to drip out."

If a **bathroom rack** comes loose, remove the screws, wrap some cotton around them, dip into glue and replace screws (or nails) in original holes. Wait until the glue is completely dry before using the rack.

From Delaware: "When I break a glass in the sink or **bathroom,** I wet a tissue or paper napkin and mop up all of those little slivers! Each little unseen sliver will stick to the wet tissue. This saves many a cut finger."

From career gal: "You can make a wonderful holder for your **bathroom brush** by cutting away the upper part of a plastic bleach container and using the lower part as a holder. This looks very neat in the bathroom, too."

FOR THAT SINKING FEELING!

From Idaho: "To keep **bathroom** surfaces bright and shiny—especially sinks and bathtubs—for the longest possible time, try the following suggestions for cleaning:

"If soap and warm water fail to remove gummy deposits, make a simple cleaning solution. Shave half a bar of naphtha-based laundry soap into a quart of warm water. Add two tablespoons of common kerosene. Apply with a rag and wash off. This usually does the trick, unless neglect has given the stain too much of a head start.

"Should the mixture fail to work, rub with a mild abrasive cleanser lightly against the stain with a coarse cloth. Use plenty of water."

From Denver: "I find that worn-out nylon hose make fine cloths to clean off **bathtub rings!** There is something about nylon that surely must be abrasive."

From Connecticut: "For those women who run out of scouring cleanser in the **bathroom,** just try using toothpaste or toothpowder (powder works best).

"This not only takes the stains away and leaves the basin gleaming, but smells nice, too. Only a very small amount is necessary."

CONTACT!

From Alaska: "Did you know that you can cover your old **bathroom scale** with contact paper?

"My scale was beat up, ten years old and rusty. I bought some contact paper and took a safety razor blade and attacked the job. Now my scale is clean and new-looking again. No more vacuuming between those dirty rubber ridges. It's waterproof, too, because I covered the bottom of the scale to prevent those miserable rust marks on my tile floor."

To find out if your **bathroom scale** is registering correctly, simply lay a five- or ten-pound bag of sugar on it.

WHERE THE IVY TWINES

For those of you who have a dreary **bathroom** and want to perk it up, have you ever tried mixing real and artificial ivy?

Or . . . if you just don't have a green thumb and can't grow philodendron and ivy, here's a cute idea that I used in my bathroom:

I bought some adhesive-backed plastic with an ivy pattern, took my scissors and cut out all the little leaves separately and stuck them on the tile wall behind the bathtub. Result? Looks like real ivy. "Growing" over that plain old tile, it gives that blank wall a finished look!

Start along the bottom of the tile above the tub and "plant" a big pot of ivy and then let the "vines" keep growing up the wall! Don't make it too perfect. It won't look real.

Now . . . around that bathroom mirror: Set a pot of *real* ivy near the sink. Then, put more "vines" up the tile wall and let them meander across the top of your mirrors! You can hardly tell where the real ivy ends and the false ivy begins. Looks as if you have a real green thumb and keeps your bathroom from appearing so bare.

If you have a wall outlet, you can cover it with big "leaves," leaving a little hole so that plug may still be used, yet disguising it beautifully.

The best part about this ivy is—it doesn't need watering and never, never dies!

BEST FOOT FORWARD

From California: "For a mother who has a **baby** with his first pair of hard-soled shoes . . . would you please allow me to tell her that this is like walking on ice for an adult?

"If these mothers will put a piece of adhesive tape on the heel and ball of the sole of the shoe, the baby will gain much confidence when he is walking. The tape keeps the child from slipping on hardwood, tile and carpeted floors, saves many bumps, and might even save some cut lips.

"This tape may be removed after the child gets used to his hard-soled shoes."

From Minnesota: "We are trying to teach our three-and-a-half-year-old **baby** daughter to put the right shoe on the right foot . . . which seems to be her greatest difficulty!

"I bought her a pair of bedroom slippers and got the bright idea of sewing one button on her right slipper.

"It works like a charm! And now I have learned to put a small piece of tape inside her right shoe only. She knows any shoe that is 'marked' goes on her right foot. No more wrong shoes or slippers for us!"

WARM-UP TIME

From North Carolina: "Instead of using a bottle warmer to warm my **baby's bottle,** I use an empty number 2½ can. I remove the label, and then I rinse the can thoroughly.

"When this can is nearly filled with hot water from the tap and put on a low flame on the stove, the bottle you put in the can will be warmed thoroughly in a very short time, as the water will come to the neck of the bottle.

"When baby starts using a full bottle of milk, change to a number 3 can (fruit juice).

"Such a can is handy to take along when traveling, too. You can fill a vacuum bottle with hot water and when the time comes to feed the infant . . . just pour the hot water in the can and the milk can be heated—without a stove!"

QUICK TRICKS

From Vermont: "If mothers would put a few agate marbles in the sterilizer with the **baby's bottles,** the bottles will come out crystal clear, and the marbles get all the corrosion."

CURL-FREE BACON

From California: "When I fry **bacon,** it does *not* curl. I fry it in my regular frying pan and place the bottom of another pan directly over the bacon itself—then put it over a very low flame. Result? Nice flat pieces of bacon and not shrunk."

A FLOURY TRIBUTE

From happy wife and cook: "Since reading the article in your column about flouring **bacon** before frying, I wouldn't serve it any other way!

"The taste is scrumptious, the grease doesn't pop one particle, and the bacon shrinks hardly a fraction of an inch. For once, there is something there when you take a bite."

All I said was: Take a piece of bacon (*not* frozen) and dip it in nothing but flour and then fry as usual. Flour gives it more body and makes a beautiful crust! Sure is good for a change.

Too, the bacon grease and brown flour make awfully good gravy.

NO STICKY STREAKS

Happy housewife from Carmel: "Here is a trick I like very much: I hold my **baking** pan upside down under hot water for a few seconds. When the pan is quite warm, I grease it with my fingers. It is always evenly greased.

"The heat of the hot water allows the shortening to flow evenly and the flour doesn't stick in streaks!"

READY BREAD

From a devoted reader: "When I buy French **bread** to use for garlic or hot-buttered bread, I slice it, butter and season it, and then slip it right back into the bag in which it came. I then put this in my freezer!

"I take out the number of pieces I need, especially when unexpected guests come, and I do not have to wait for that frozen slab to thaw before slicing it. All I need to do is separate the pieces and heat them. Thus they can be served with a minimum of trouble."

BOUILLON MAKES IT BETTER

A mother of a large family writes: "When I make a pot of soup, I take out the soup bone and add a couple of beef **bouillon** cubes. When I make chicken and dumplings, I always add at least one chicken bouillon cube to the chicken stock. I also add a chicken bouillon cube to chicken cream gravy when making it, and this always improves the flavor."

When **butter** is too cold to spread, turn a hot bowl over it and it will barely soften, but not melt. Your bowl can be made warm by filling it with hot water from your tap for a few minutes.

A BEDTIME STORY

Many of us have king-sized **beds.** Many of us have twin beds that are pushed together.

But my husband is big—six feet two and weights 200 pounds. Me? Five feet two and 105. Two three-quarter beds, pushed together and dressed as one bed, was the answer for us. And I found an inexpensive way to dress our big bed!

Comforters are the most expensive items for a bed like this. Also, when it comes time to launder most comforters, what a mess! They are too big to fit into the washing or dry-cleaning machines. So, I bought *two* twin-sized comforters (got 'em on sale) and went to the slipcover section in a department store and bought strips of snaps (they look like grippers and are used on slipcovers in place of zippers). These snaps come on cotton tape and I sewed one strip on the side of each comforter.

This allows me to snap the two single comforters together beautifully. When the comforters are ready for laundry or dry cleaning, I just unsnap them. Also, the center where they are snapped together shows me where the center of the bed is, and I get the comforter on evenly.

There's no doubt about it, when a woman decides to splurge and buy king-sized beds, she sure has her problems. Bedding seems to cost as much as the beds themselves!

I took my contour sheets and used them as they were. I dressed the mattresses on the beds separately, but sewed the top sheets together! This makes one big draw sheet.

My next expense was pillows. I never thought about that when I bought the beds.

First I bought king-sized pillows. Then I had no pillowcases to fit! Another expense.

It finally dawned on this bird brain of mine to use three regular-sized pillows! They're great! You can use all your same pillowslips—*plus* you have an extra pillow on the bed at all times.

This has saved us many arguments. The third pillow can be used while reading, watching TV, or for propping yourself up anytime, and it fits right in the center of the bed when you make it up. This removes that ugly indentation in the center of the bed.

Now for the bedspread. Some king-sized bedspreads (and, gals, a queen-sized one just won't fit! I tried to save that way, too) have extra yardage in them. Buy one. It's worth the extra few cents you pay.

I bought chenille. It can be tumbled in the drier to remove

the dust, doesn't show soil easily. . . . and means less trouble when you're making the bed because, somehow, an inch off on either side just doesn't look too bad.

Did anyone ever hear of chenille lamp shades before? Try them. They are easy to make, and your mistakes don't show. The thickness of the material hides all the big stitches.

After all, most lamp shades in the bedroom need covering anyway. If we had an extra few dollars for lamp shades . . . we would replace the ones in the living room!

I cut about eighteen inches off the top of the bedspread and used the material to cover my bedside lamp shades! Darling!

The shades, when covered with chenille, give soft lighting to the bedroom (good for TV and the nights when you want to read and your husband wants to sleep).

Those of you who have regular-sized beds, think about buying a larger bedspread next time and cutting off some of the material, then covering your lamp shades or a few pillows with it so they will match.

And gals, if you have a bunch of floor pillows, couch pillows or outside patio pillows and couches to slipcover, think about buying a chenille bedspread. But . . . be sure to watch for one on sale so you can save that way.

WHEN YOUR TROUBLES ARE SPREADING!

From Louisiana: "Every morning I seem to put my heavy throw **bedspread** on twice! First the wrong way, then the right way. I have solved this by marking the back of the bedspread with a pencil, making arrows that point toward the head of the bed for the top."

From Texas: "When making our **beds** I smooth out the spread with the long, flat, bottom side of a wire coat hanger. I find this much easier than stretching across the bed."

From Missouri: "For years I have used hobnail **bedspreads**. Once in a while one of these little devils (a hob) will come loose and you will think your bedspread is ruined . . . but it isn't.

"Take a big embroidery needle, thread it with two strands of matching thread and just pull it through four or five times in the place where the tuft is missing. Cut the threads in two, and tamp the new tuft into place to match the others."

From Cleveland: "My husband smokes in bed. He recently burned some holes in the top of a beautiful, brand new, dark-blue taffeta *bedspread.* I am exasperated. I know the holes cannot be patched or mended without leaving a pucker that will show. And you know this type of bedspread has a white cotton batting filler which shows through when a hole occurs. Now what can I do?"

The exact same thing happened in our house! Here's what I did:

I took a felt marker—same color as my bedspread. They can be bought at any dime store and most drug stores. I gently touched the tiny holes where the white cotton showed through. The marker dyed the white cotton.

And you were right about tacking and sewing up those holes. It looks horrible.

Don't use too much dye. You don't want the dye to get all over the spread and leave a ring. You might prefer to use a toothpick with a dab of cotton on the end and some ink as a substitute for the above method.

TWO FOR THE TIME OF ONE

A woman from New Hampshire has a suggestion for an easy way to iron **bedsheets:** "Fold a sheet in quarters, put it across your ironing board and iron or press your other garments right on top.

"Keep turning the sheet as you iron other garments and all that has to be done to finish is to iron the hem. You will find that your sheets will be ironed better than if ironed alone.

"You can iron pillowcases this way, also. It not only saves time, but a portion of the electric bill, too."

USE COOLER WATER FOR PASTELS

From Oregon: "For those who have colored **bedsheets:** White sheets can be washed in hot water from 140 degrees to 160 degrees, but pastels should not be washed in water over 120 degrees.

"Another thing, use only half as much bleach for colored sheets as for white sheets. This is advice from the manufacturer."

A NEEDLE IN A SHEET-STACK

From Los Angeles: "When fitted bottom **bedsheets** need mending because of rips on the edges, use a piece of knitted cotton (such as the tail of a T-shirt) to mend the sheet. This material allows a small amount of stretch, and the weakened spot won't tear out again near the mending when you are pulling the sheet to get the last fitted corner over the mattress!"

From Delaware: "If you have fitted **bedsheets** which are just a little too tight to fit on your bed, rip the contour seam open and insert the leg part of an old white ribbed sock and stitch it back again. This 'gives' just enough to allow you to slip the sheet over the mattress easily.

"Sometimes more than one corner will have to be done. I find it best to put these insertions in diagonally opposite corners. Usually two insertions is all it takes. They keep your sheets from splitting, too."

From Michigan: "I inherited a number of odd-sized **bedsheets.** Since my mattresses were two different sizes, I made my own contour sheets.

"I placed the sheet evenly on the mattress and tucked it in on all sides, then carefully pinned *each corner* together. I removed it, and, after sewing a row of stitches diagonally, on each corner, I tried the sheet on the bed again. It seemed to fit, so I removed the pins and sewed it a second time, making a flat fell or French seam.

"I then sewed a piece of colored bias tape (to match the

room) in one corner of each sheet so that I could easily identify the right sheet for the right mattress.

"After the first sheet for each bed is completed, save the corner that you cut out and use it for a pattern. Then it will not be necessary to measure every sheet."

Patterns are wonderful, but they do not fit all sizes of mattresses . . . or so I found out! Here's how I made my own contour sheets:

As my mattresses varied in size, I found it far better to do just what the lady from Michigan suggested. I placed the sheet (after washing, because some sheets shrink) on top of my mattress, and holding each corner out at a 45-degree angle, took some straight pins and pinned the corners to the exact size of the mattress.

I followed her instructions and tried the sheet back on the bed before finishing the underneath corners. When I was sure it fitted, I finished the sheet by inserting elastic on *opposite corners* (two insertions of elastic instead of the regular four, thus saving on elastic).

I also discovered an easier way to make up the bed for those who have twin-sized mattresses pushed together to form a king-sized bed:

If you have never found a contour sheet to fit an *over-sized* bed, instead of making twin-sized sheets to cover each mattress, make a contour sheet to fit the *entire* expanse of the two beds.

Rather than putting the sheet on all four corners of each mattress (which makes eight times), it is far easier to apply it to only four corners. This cuts your work in exactly half. Think that over!

Also, instead of washing two bottom sheets each week, you'll only be washing one! For those who send their linens to commercial laundries, you may be charged a wee bit more for a king-sized sheet, but it is cheaper than paying for two separate sheets.

Where can you get your material? Buy a big sheet (or sheeting) and turn it *sideways* (this means the exact wrong way across the bed), and continue from there to custom-make your own sheets.

If you will look in your closet and find your favorite contour sheet, you may easily rip (this means to remove the thread) from one corner of this "pet" sheet, and press it flat on your ironing board. Then, you will have a perfect pattern for your individual contour sheets. Later, the sheet may be resewn. Lay newspaper beneath this sheet and take a crayon and draw around the pattern, then take your scissors and cut it out. And use that pattern on those new sheets you are cutting.

For those of you who are copying sheets with insertions, the part cut from the corner of the sheet will suffice for your insertion.

Some sheets have reinforced gussets. If your sheet was hard to fit on the bed, instead of using a reinforced cloth gusset, try putting some elastic in these corners! It gives just enough to keep from breaking your fingernails, lifting that heavy mattress, putting your knee under it and "splitting your insides" trying to pull it over the fourth corner!

SPRING CLEANING!

From Montana: "After years in the housekeeping business, I have found that if I take an old mattress cover or contour sheet and slip it over my coil-type **bedsprings,** it eliminates all dusting. It also protects the mattress from possible rust.

"To prevent the coils from making a mark on your mattress, you can put an old quilt or blanket—and some even use newspapers—underneath the contour sheet or mattress cover.

"If you do not have an old contour sheet or mattress cover, don't go buy one! You can use any old regular type of sheet. Take some safety pins if you cannot sew, and pin the sheet to the coil itself!"

From Connecticut: "One day when I was cleaning the **bedsprings** my husband watched me for a minute and then asked, 'Why don't we take them outside at house-cleaning time and just hose them down with a garden hose?'

"We did, and the springs dried in fifteen minutes. I am so delighted with this idea that I just wanted to pass it on."

CRADLE TALK

From Alaska: "I made a mattress cover for my **baby's crib** by sewing two fitted crib sheets together on three sides. Slip it on like a pillowcase. Now his sheet stays on, but good."

From Pennsylvania: "Husband got a pair of old suspenders? They make wonderful fasteners for **baby's crib** sheet and blankets.

"Put the suspender itself under the mattress and bring the clasps to the edge of the bed to hold the covers. They can be easily removed when dressing or changing baby or the bed."

When I replace our worn-out twin fitted sheets for my children's **bed,** I rip off the top of the sheet and sew in two yards of 36-inch percale *print*. My girls absolutely love them!

For the boys' rooms, I use stripes or boys' prints.

From North Dakota: "When making the children's **beds,** I put the length of the sheets and blankets crosswise on their beds. They need not be tucked in at the feet and this gives me much more room to tuck in on each side.

"Helps keep the children from getting uncovered and also from falling out of bed! Children are so small their feet never come to the end of the bed like grown persons, so why waste all that sheet on the tuck-under at the bottom?"

From Kentucky: "When I need sheets for my **baby's bassinet,** I make pillowslips from embossed plisse, long enough to fold the top under about four inches and pin on the underneath side of the bassinet pillow. I pin rubber sheeting around the bassinet mattress and then put on my pillowslip. When baby spits up on them, these slips may be washed and no ironing is required.

"After the baby has outgrown the bassinet, the rubber sheeting can be cut to fit inside of the pillowslip, and put on the crib crossways under the baby, with enough excess to tuck under the sides.

"By putting the rubber inside the pillowslip, Mother saves

changing sheets and laundering them. The plisse pillowslip is easy and quick to remove and washes beautifully. It looks much nicer than a plain rubber sheet on a baby bed."

YES, YOU CAN WASH WOOL BLANKETS—BUT . . .

I am besieged with letters wanting to know how to wash a wool **blanket** in a washing machine. Here's the best way I have found, after much research and trying to do it myself.

If you have a drier, put your blanket in it and let it tumble *without* heat for a few minutes. This is the first most important step. Here's why:

The tumbling will shake out most of the loose dust and dirt. *Never, never,* put any liquids on something that is dusty. This will cause more spots. If you do not have a drier, take the blanket outside and shake it hard to remove this loose dirt and then dust or brush it with a brush.

Mix some water with a bit of good detergent in a small bowl. Pre-treat the soiled spots with a soft brush which has been dipped in this detergent mixture.

Fill your washing machine with some lukewarm water and add three-fourths to one cup of the same brand of detergent you used to pre-treat the blanket. Do *not* add your blanket at this time. Turn your washer on and let it run a full three minutes so that the detergent is thoroughly dissolved. Then either turn off or unplug your washing machine.

Put the dust-free blanket, which has been pre-treated, into the washing machine and let it soak for ten to fifteen minutes (not more than fifteen minutes, ladies). Do *not* turn the washing machine on, because you do not want it to agitate. The agitator in a washing machine causes the little particles of wool to rub against one another. This is called "felting" and it is the one thing you want to avoid.

Use a new "plumbers' friend" and plunge the blanket up and down in the water for a minute or so. Pick up the blanket and turn it over a few times. Remember this water is *not* hot; it is only lukewarm, so your hands can stand that treatment.

Then plug in your washing machine again—remember to do this before fifteen minutes—turning it to "spin dry" this time, and let all of the soiled water drain out. If you do not have a spin-drier machine, loosen the wringer on your wringer-type of washing machine, fold the blanket carefully and run it through the wringer.

Fill the washing machine with lukewarm water once more, and soak the blanket another ten minutes or so, using your plunger again. Do *not* use your agitator. Never at any time when washing a wool blanket do we turn on the agitating process. Let your washing machine drain again.

Then, after the blanket has spun dry, remove it and fill the washer a third time with warm water and add one-half a cup of vinegar. Put your blanket back in and let it soak about five minutes. Take that old plunger and plunge that blanket up and down. Let it spin dry once more. The vinegar water need not be rinsed out. When the blanket is thoroughly dry you will have no vinegar odor.

I don't think there's anything like a drier for drying blankets, but I *never* put a wool blanket in a drier by itself. I always put four or five clean bath towels in the drier first, then turn on the drier and let it heat the bath towels and tumble them for about five minutes.

Then is the time to put your blanket in the drier with the bath towels. The bath towels will act as a buffer and brush against the fibers of the wool blanket, making them fluffy. Too, the bath towels will absorb the excess moisture and keep your blankets from getting *too* dry! This is exactly what we are looking for. Never *overdry* a wool blanket. Let the drier run about twenty minutes.

Remove your blanket from the drier while it is still slightly damp. Stretch the blanket out (if possible, in the fresh air), and then let it finish drying. It may be hung over two clotheslines.

After the blanket is dry, lay it across a table and brush it well with a whiskbroom or a clean vegetable brush. If neither of these is available, wash your hairbrush and use it.

All that is left to do is press the binding with a slightly warm iron and put your clean blanket back on the bed.

Keep your blankets clean, gals. They last longer.

From New Jersey: "Every year, after washing my **blankets**, I add a cup of mothballs to the rinse water. The mothballs dissolve in the warm water, thus distributing evenly among the blankets. This gives them storage protection."

BEWARE WHEN USING BLEACH

A lady from Minneapolis asked what caused small holes in her linens. Some of the linens were less than two months old.

I have taken this up with the president of a leading laundry association. He has had home economists do research, and here is the answer as far as we know:

The first opinion is that the customer has misused **bleach.** Household bleaches used full strength for cleaning purposes can seriously weaken the fibers in a cleaning cloth or dishrag unless the bleach is thoroughly rinsed out. Furthermore, other fabrics that come in contact with the unrinsed cleaning cloth can also be damaged.

For example, if you pour pure household bleach on your dishcloth for bleaching your sink then drop it into a laundry hamper or a laundry bag, any fabric that comes in contact with this cleaning cloth will be weakened by the remaining bleach.

This cloth may stay in your laundry hamper for a few days. It is impossible to see what damage it has done to other fibers which have been in contact with the cleaning cloth until it is washed! Then, perhaps, when the linen is washed, the weak fibers in your sheets will crumple and float way, leaving little holes and tiny tears. Your washcloth will have more damage, but this is not too important, because it costs only a few cents. And your sheets were quite expensive.

Check up on how you use your bleach and see if you are following the directions on the bottle or box.

Another thing that causes holes in laundry—you just might happen to have a rough spot in either your washing machine or the drier, and that will cause snagging and damage, too. And be sure never to overload your machine.

FOR THE BIRDS!

Did you know that those big plastic bleach blottles you usually throw away when empty make wonderful **bird houses?**

Here's all you do:

Rinse the bottle out carefully and discard the cap. The cap is discarded so that odor from the bacteria which might collect inside where the birds gather can have an escape hatch.

The top is so narrow that even heavy rains cannot get into the bottle.

The next thing to do is cut two or three small holes in the bottom of the bottle. This allows for any moisture which might collect in the bottle to drop through. Take a sharp knife and cut at least two holes on each side of the bottle about the size of a silver dollar. These two holes give the birds cross-ventilation.

All that is left to do is to hang the plastic bird house on the branch of a tree. The handle of the bottle will fit over the branch stub.

Those who do not want to cut a stem or branch of the tree to hang the bottle on can easily put a cord through the handle and tie it to any branch of the tree.

HOW ABOUT A "BLOTTER BLOUSE"?

Housewives wear slacks, pedal pushers, skirts and shorts when they clean house. But these items don't seem to create the laundry and ironing problem that blouses do.

You can put on a clean **blouse** in the morning and by noon it will look as if it had been worn three days! Splashes from dishwashing or cleaning the bathroom, plus the spatters at the stove, are what get blouses dirty.

I made "cleaning blouses" out of some bath towels and they are wonderful for blotting up the spots and spatters. The spots don't show, the blouses require no ironing, perspiration absorbs quickly without leaving a ring, and they always look nice. Plus all that, they're really comfortable!

These sack blouses can be made in about ten minutes. They

can be worn with anything, are cool in the summer and warm in the winter, and can be topped with a sweater when it's extra chilly.

Just take a bath towel, fold in half, cut a hole for the neck, turn neck opening under and stitch about three times (or bind) and sew the sides up, leaving room for the arm opening! That's all. (Women with large chest measurements might want to add side darts.)

Neck lines may be round or square. Or "V" type! I personally like the "V" type best. They are easier to make and hang on the shoulders better. Be sure to make the hole for the neck big enough so that it will slide over your head when you have all those rollers and pincurls in your hair!

If you want to make the blouse exceptionally pretty, the edges of the sleeve opening may be turned under and stitched a few times. This adds a professional touch. The quickest and easiest way to hem the sleeve opening is to do it *before* you sew the sides up. Try leaving the sides open about four inches from the bottom for an oriental look.

After making five of these "cleaning blouses," I would like to pass on a few more hints before you indulge.

Don't go and buy an expensive heavy bath towel. I did, and that was a mistake! It is too heavy, doesn't hang as easily as a used one . . . and besides, you need the new towel in your linen stock.

New and heavy bath towels do not absorb perspiration, nor do they dry as fast as old ones. You want to be able to wipe your hands on the blouse when the phone rings and you are in the midst of dishwashing. Also, heavy bath towels take up more room in the washing machine (cost more to send out, too!), and it takes more soap and water to launder them.

If you must buy a towel to make a blouse, be sure it is cheap, thin and on sale! Watch for a bargain. You're not going to wear your cleaning blouse to a bridge party or a church social.

The best thing I found was . . . *pockets!* Put pockets in your cleaning blouse. The more the better. They will save many steps in the long run. Pockets hold tissues, your package of cigarettes, lighters, the pencil Dad used for the crossword puzzle last night and left on the table . . . just about anything.

If you want lots of pockets, the easiest way to make them is to turn up one end of the towel about four inches before you start (there is no right and wrong side to most towels) and stitch pockets. Make three in front of the blouse. This also gives the blouse style and allows one extra pocket. Bind or turn under and stitch on machine a few times. Or stitch washcloths to the towel to make pockets.

Your cleaning blouses may be fitted, belted or have buttons added . . . if you are THAT ambitious! But, plain or fancy, they are wonderful for housework, yardwork, baking, doing laundry, and for gals who come home from the office to cook supper.

These towels make good garments for the kiddies, too! Either male or female, and at any age. Make shorts to match them.

Take one old bath towel and try. What can you lose? You'll love it.

BOBBY PIN MARKS THE SPOT

From a gentleman reader: "I find that the best bookmark I have ever come across is a **bobby pin.** Just slide it along the edge of any book or periodical you happen to be reading. This not only allows identification for the page you are reading, but . . . you can put the bobby pin at exactly the paragraph you stopped at!"

WHEN BUBBLE GUM TROUBLES YOU!

From Pennsylvania: "Having three kids in our family who are addicted to **bubble gum,** I had quite a problem getting this out when it became tangled in their hair. It was especially difficult with the girls, who had long hair.

"One day a friend handed me a jar of cold cream—the kind any woman should have around the house—and told me to try it. I put some on the tangled mess of gum and hair, rubbed it in well and then took a dry rag and pulled down on the strands of hair several times. Sure enough, the gum completely vanished. There was no sign of it at all, not even on the rag.

"This trick certainly is a boon to me. Now I don't have to cut the gum out of their hair and leave those ugly gaps!"

"PRETTY BUBBLES IN THE AIR . . . !"

From Philadelphia: "We make soap-**bubble** mixture for our children by shaving two ounces of good bar soap. We personally use castile soap. Put this in a pint fruit jar and fill it with water which has been boiled and allowed to cool. Shake it thoroughly and allow to stand until the top of the water becomes clear. Pour off the clear water (the soap will have settled to the bottom by this time). We then add a few spoons of glycerine. A little vegetable coloring even makes it better, so the kiddies say."

This recipe has been checked with the Poison Control Center and the Board of Health and it is quite safe. If you do not have bubble blowers, use a straw or the wooden spool from a spool of thread. Works just as well!

And did you know that you can take an empty spool, dampen it, rub one end on a soft bar of soap and then blow, and it makes real nice bubbles for a child? Let him do it while he is taking his bath. I used to do this when I was a kid. My, but that was a long time ago!

SWEET SOMETHINGS!

From Montana: "When giving the children a birthday party, I buy flat-bottomed ice cream cones. I then use my favorite **cake** dough and fill them from one-half to three-fourths full and bake them in the ice cream cups in a slow oven on a cookie sheet.

"These may be iced with a regular icing and—with a decorator—each child's name can be put on the top of the iced 'ice cream cone.' When the children are ready to be seated, let them find their own names! They love it."

From North Carolina: "I baked a **cake** and decided to wait until morning to frost it. I left it in the pan, and when I got ready to frost it, the cake wouldn't come loose from the pan.

"My mother suggested that I put it in a 'low' oven for a few minutes. It worked like a charm."

From Nevada: "I spread my leftover cake icing between graham crackers. They make real tasty sandwich cookies for the kiddies. They may also be frozen for future use."

THE MORE BUTTERY, THE BETTER!

From New York: "For those who like to eat **corn** on the cob, try buttering the corn in this fashion:

"If you have corn holders, use them. Then, holding each end of the corn, roll it back and forth on a quarter-pound stick of butter or margarine before serving it!

"This does mess up the stick of butter but it can be used later when cooking. For those who do not have corn holders, make your own with toothpicks. You can use the key from the end of a coffee or shortening can for corn holders, too.

"I found that when the butter or margarine was put on the ear of corn right after the ear was removed from the pot, it kept the kernels from shrinking!"

From Maryland: "While cleaning some **corn** on the cob, I became so disgusted with trying to pick off the corn silk that I grabbed a dampened paper towel. I brushed downward on the ear of corn with it and every strand came off!"

NO NEED TO RACK YOUR BRAINS

From a reader: "For those who don't have a cooling rack for icing **cookies and cakes,** there's no need to buy one.

"Just remove the broiler rack from your oven before heating the stove and lay a thin cloth over it. Set your cake to cool on this after baking."

CAN THOSE COOKIES!

From a cookie canner: "I always make a batch of **cookie dough** and put it in frozen-juice cans, then put the cans in my freezer. (I only make cookie batter when I am in the mood.)

"When I want to bake cookies, I take the can of frozen dough, open the other end and push the dough through the can.

"Slice with a sharp knife, place on tray covered with foil and bake."

NO TOUGH COOKIES!

From Maine: "I seldom make rolled **cookies** because I hate the way they get tough when I work the dough in the flour to roll them. But I just made a marvelous discovery!

"Mix half flour and half sugar and sprinkle this mixture on your pastry cloth or dough board and then roll the cookies. They roll *faster* and *easier* and the little bit of sugar that is absorbed offsets the toughening action of the flour and the handling.

"Because I dislike the job of making cookies, I have learned to make more than one batch at one time. I save the rolled-type cookies to bake last. I roll these and cut them as rapidly as possible, putting one panful of cookies on a sheet of wax paper and stacking them in layers to fit the cookie sheet until I have them all rolled and cut.

"While the last of the cookies are baking, I can clean the kitchen. If you are interrupted or don't have time to finish baking them, pop the sheets of wax paper (which are filled with cut dough) in your freezer; they are much more apt to get baked tomorrow and far better than a lump of sticky dough in the refrigerator, which usually gets dried out and hard.

"The flour and sugar mixture has another advantage:

"Just turn the cookies over as you place them on the pan and they have a daintily sugared top, eliminating the mess of trying to put sugar on a cookie so that it will not get on the pan and burn."

A CEREAL STORY

From Delaware: "My four children all love hot oatmeal **cereal** for breakfast but my eighteen-month-old daughter made such a mess eating hers that I almost hated to fix it every morning.

"As I usually have my hands full feeding my four-month-old baby, I could not feed my toddler at the same time, and she does not handle a spoon too gracefully. I hit upon the idea of mixing her cereal in a plastic glass and now she 'drinks' her oatmeal and no more mess."

From Oregon: "When I cook hot **cereal** for our children, before dishing the cereal up in bowls, I mix the butter, sugar and cream right in the saucepan while the cereal is still on the stove.

"Anyone with small children will find this method just wonderful. There is no mess at the table and no fighting over which child has the sugar. No spilled cereal over the sides of the bowl, either, while stirring it!"

From Pennsylvania: "When cooking cornmeal for breakfast **cereal** or other uses, mix the cornmeal with *cold* water *before* stirring it into the boiling water and it does not get lumpy."

From Virginia: "I am eleven years old and love to cook. I get tired of eating the same things all the time and can imagine other children do, too.

"I found that if you add food coloring to oatmeal or grits, etc., it looks like a brand new **cereal!** I do not advise using green with oatmeal as it tends to look very sickening; however, the yellow or pink is beautiful."

I have used food coloring in rice and cream-of-wheat. I put it in the water before I dump in the **cereal.**

I mixed two drops of yellow food coloring with a drop of red and got a beautiful orange in my cream-of-wheat! The orange coloring reminds me of oranges. The yellow reminds me of golden old-fashioned wheat.

Try it! You don't have anything to lose but a couple of drops of coloring.

FIVE-MINUTE RECIPE FOR INSTANT COFFEE

Here's a cutie-pie for those of you who drink cups and cups of instant **coffee** with instant (or powdered) cream and sugar.

We open three things each time we make a cup. The jar of coffee, the instant cream and the sugar bowl.

That's three lids screwed and unscrewed each time we make a cup of java. Plus . . . three spoons. (Can't possibly put the coffee spoon in the cream. Or the cream spoon in the sugar or vice-versa.)

Here's what I did:

I took one jar and mixed my own favorite flavoring. As I use one heaping teaspoon of coffee, one level teaspoon of sugar and one level teaspoon of instant cream in each cup, I poured one cup of instant coffee into a big fruit jar, with one-half cup of powered cream and one-half cup of sugar.

I shook the jar well to mix it thoroughly.

I poured this into small jars and set them in the most convenient place in my kitchen.

Now, when I need that cup o' java . . . I just open *one* jar, dip out the special mixture, and look at all the energy I have saved!

See how much faster this is and count up the seconds you will save on each cup of coffee. Multiply that by the cups of coffee you drink each day (see how many seconds you save there!), then multiply that by the days in each year (most times it's 365!).

This also works with instant tea, which I drink each afternoon.

When you mix your coffee, if you don't use cream it still pays to mix the sugar with the coffee, or if you don't use sugar, it still pays to mix the cream, etc. It always saves time.

SHE LEARNS INSTANTLY

A new bride writes: "Did you know you could make instant **coffee** in an automatic electric percolator?

"Just add the water and instant coffee without the coffee basket or stem. Reasons for doing this might be:

"To keep instant coffee hot after making it (this is my reason), or to fool someone into thinking he is drinking real coffee! Perhaps a husband who is not supposed to have caffeine or a husband who *thinks* he does not like instant coffee!"

CARPET CUES

From Michigan: "For women who have wall-to-wall **carpeting:** Ever fret over how to vacuum right up to the walls and corners where the carpeting meets the baseboard?

"I have a very small nylon brush which looks like a miniature whisk broom and, in fact, was intended as a clothes brush. It fits onto the cord rack of my vacuum cleaner and hangs there as a permanent attachment, always ready when I need it to whisk out those areas so hard to get at.

"This gets every bit of dust and lint and the tiny particles that seem to want to hide in the cracks against the walls and corners."

From Vermont: "If our vacuum cleaner cannot reach the stairs, and especially if they are **carpeted** . . . rip up some old newspapers. Wet them and squeeze them out thoroughly.

"Scatter the wet pieces of paper on the top steps and begin sweeping both the paper and dust downstairs. The dust particles will stick on the dampened newspapers."

LADIES, BE SEATED!

Let's talk about re-covering our dining-room **chairs.** You can do it yourself. It's inexpensive, it's easy, and it's quick.

All you have to do is turn each chair upside down, remove the little screws in each corner and the seat comes loose. Remove it and lay it on your material and draw a pattern, allowing a few inches to turn under.

If you have a stapler, use it. It's great and quicker than a hammer and tacks and saves mashed fingers. If you don't have one, use your hammer to tack the material to the bottom of the seat. Replace the seat and screws and presto . . . it's beautiful!

If the dining-room chairs have cushioned backs, I have found it best to pull the gimp loose, since it is usually glued on. Either remove the old material from the back, or cut a pattern by holding a piece of foil over the material and mashing it with your fingernail. A perfect pattern will result. Make your pattern and then cut your material. Replace on chair back and either tack or staple the fabric to it.

Replace the same gimp with some good glue. It is not necessary to buy new gimp. It usually lasts for years and years.

I do not always rip off the old upholstery material on my dining-room chairs. I just apply the new material over the old. This gives more cushion.

But . . . and here's the real tip-off . . . when you are re-covering these chairs, put two pieces of fabric over each seat!

Here's why: The seat of the chair always gets soiled before the back does—probably about twice as fast. So, when the seat cover becomes so soiled that it must be replaced again (you may not be able to match your material) . . . just remove the top cover!

I've found that the soil will work down through the top layer just enough so that when the top cover is ripped off, the second cover will exactly match the back of the chair.

So look for some fabric on sale and re-cover your dining room chairs. And it's worth the few extra dollars to get enough material to cover the seats twice.

PERK UP THAT CHINTZ

A friend wanted to know how to rejuvenate **chintz** bedspreads and curtains. I ironed mine with the right side down on a sheet of waxed paper. It adds shine and body to the material.

Once your chintz has become limp, this method is sure worth trying. After all, tallow is included even in some of the starches we *cook*—the contents listed on some boxes say so!

I suggest that you never use bleach on chintz. Although the manufacturers do not tell you this, after inquiring from clothing manufacturers, I have learned that this should never be done.

SAVE, SAVE, SAVE . . .

From Kansas: "When you buy a new can of **cleanser**, copper cleaner, etc., remove the square piece of sticky paper that covers the four holes and stick it back on top of the can, leaving only two holes open.

"It's easier to regulate the amount you use and it saves a good deal of the cleanser, because you never apply too much this way."

CLOCK-WORK

From New York: "Half the confusion in the mornings at our house has been cut by the installation of a **clock** in the bathroom. It does away with dilly-dallying in the tub, in the shower, and over hair-combing! Each member of the family is limited to a set time."

BRIGHTEN CHANDELIERS

From California: "When my dining-room **chandeliers** get coated with fly specks, I find I can remove them by sponging the chandelier with alcohol. I rinse this with soap suds and then polish dry. The real secret is: When you polish, put a little oil on your cloth and the fly specks won't stick again."

A man from Chicago writes: "Here is a helpful hint for folks who like to enjoy the sparkle of crystal **chandeliers** but dread the job of taking them apart for cleaning.

"I use a tall, narrow jar—such as olives come in—and fill it one-half inch from the top with a strong solution of detergent and hot water. I then place newspapers on a table beneath the crystal fixture, and, holding this jar under the crystal lobes and prisms, I run the jar well up and around each chain of crystal drops! The grime drops off and falls back into the jar.

"I do this twice with my mixture of detergent and then take another bottle with clear, warm water and rinse the same way, letting the drops of water fall on the newspaper which has been placed on the table. I have found that rather hot water with the detergent works best."

Dear ladies: Just because this man has found an excellent way to do the teardrops *does not* mean that you should take a big tub of water and douse the entire chandelier in it! Remember, this gadget does contain electricity!

A friend of mine has one of these chandeliers hanging in her dining room. We unscrewed the light bulbs and gently lifted the crystal saucer—which also contained a batch of prisms and teardrops—and doused the entire saucer with all its little gadgets into a pan of sudsy water to which some ammonia had been added. We then poured water over this little saucer which we held over an empty pan. This removed most of the accumulated dirt.

On the parts which we did not remove, the gentleman's explanation was absolutely excellent and, sir, we thank you.

AND . . . "IT GIVES A LOVELY LIGHT!"

From New York: "Recently I had a meeting in my home and a number of the gals smoked. They were surprised that I kept **candles** lighted and asked that I write to tell you that where there is a lot of smoking going on, a candle kept burning will burn up the smoke! If it is a large room, you may wish to burn more than one candle."

WHEN YOU'RE BURNING THAT CANDLE

From Virginia: "We like to dine by candlelight. Sometimes the **candles** are too small for the candelabra. Just wrap and crush some foil around the base of the candle and put it in its holder."

From California: "Dip the base of a **candle** in hot water before placing it in candelabra. This makes it fit and stick better."

From Montreal: "I put my **candelabra** under the hot water faucet in my kitchen sink and just let the water run slowly over the holders to remove all the wax. There is no effort on my part! I always replace my candles while the holders are still warm, as this gives them a better anchor. They seem to melt slightly and always stand straight."

When pouring hot water over the **candelabra** to remove the wax, be sure to line the kitchen sink! Otherwise you might have a plumbing bill!

From Colorado: "I have found that if I keep my **candles** in the refrigerator a few days before a party they do not drip so badly. 'Dripless' candles do drip, you know! I believe a draft causes that."

DOING IS BELIEVING

A woman wrote to me recently that she washed her black **crepe** dresses in her washing machine *without* using any soap or detergent. All she used was ammonia and water.

This was mighty hard for me to believe. Now I not only believe her, but I thank her. Last year I bought a black crepe dress. I don't know whether the material is rayon, nylon, or a blend. Since I only buy one new black dress about every two years, I was very hesitant to try her method of home laundry on it!

However, the cleaners made a mistake. When it came back from the cleaners this time, I knew that it had been wet-washed. It still had wrinkles in it. And the dress had shine all over the front. Nothing makes black crepe look so shabby as shine.

I knew I could remove the shine by dipping a wash cloth in pure vinegar, wringing it out and rubbing it over the shiny portion, but figuring you all love me as much as I love you, I thought I would experiment with *my* dress.

I filled my washing machine with *lukewarm* water. I have a top-loading type of machine. If you have the other type, I would suggest that before you place your garment in the machine, you fill it with cold water, then add a little bit of hot water. *Never* put a black crepe dress in hot water.

I then added one-half cup of ammonia, turned on the machine and let it run a minute or two so the water and ammonia were well mixed. Then put in the dress—*nothing* else.

Ladies, I don't have one of these fancy machines with a lot of buttons. Mine is a semi-automatic. So I ran the machine about four minutes, opened the top of the machine and took the dress out and held it in my hand while letting the water drip out of it. I then drained and rinsed the machine thoroughly with my hose, and refilled the machine with more lukewarm water. I added one-half cup of vinegar, put the dress back into the machine and let it rinse for another three minutes. I did not let the dress spin dry. I decided that this was where the cleaners must have made their mistake, because spin-drying does cause wrinkles.

Before the machine started to spin, I removed the dress, dripping wet, turned it wrong side out and put it on a plastic coat hanger. I then hung it in the sun.

Ladies, my crepe dress is about the prettiest that it has ever been. Granted, all of the shine was not off, but a few rubs with good old down-to-earth vinegar, and what little shine was left was removed immediately. And this is most important . . . I found that my black dress was also wrinkle-free! It did not even need touching up with an iron! Why? I have no idea. It might have been the type of material. What I really think it was . . . is that I took it from the lukewarm water and hung it in the warm sun.

Gals, this is hard to believe. I didn't believe it myself. I am not telling you to go stick your best black crepe dress in the washing machine, but if the dress is in bad shape anyway— shiny, wrinkled, soiled—why not take a chance?

If I were you, I would not try to press the dress myself if you find that it does need a pressing job. Send it to the cleaners and say: "Press only."

Now, about the belt. Some belts have some type of lining on the inside. I do not recommend putting belts into the washing machine. In fact, I didn't even take a chance on my own!

Belts on black dresses seldom get dirty—and if they do, the dirt doesn't show anyway—so what I did was dip my wash-cloth in my plain old vinegar, wring it out well and just rub the belt thoroughly with it. This not only removed all shine, but the belt looks as good as new.

CARPET YOUR COASTERS!

Iced-tea glasses and **coasters** have been the bane of my existence for years! No matter how good they seem to be, the water always accumulates in the coaster itself, so that when the glass is picked up, it still drips.

Now, what good is a coaster if you are still going to get water on the front of your dress and across your tables?

I've got the answer to this. Recently I was testing pieces of carpet for burns, wax spots, etc., when I accidentally put one piece of carpet in a little tray that sits on our end table. That night my husband said: "Well, Heloise, I see you've finally found something that takes the 'sweat' off my glass."

I didn't even know what he meant! He thought I had pasted the piece of carpet in the little tray where he usually puts his glass.

Since then I have taken my coasters and cut round circles of old carpet to fit the bottom of each one of them—and glued them in! Ladies, they are absolutely terrific.

When the glass sweats now, the carpeting absorbs all of the moisture. So when the glass is lifted, there's no dripping at all.

This is wonderful for those of you who have scraps left over from wall-to-wall carpeting. They look nice in your living room, too, especially if they do happen to match or contrast with your carpeting.

Why not give it a whirl? You have nothing to lose except a few inches of carpet, a minute of your time and a dab of glue.

From Long Island: "Many people get water marks on their furniture caused by moisture from flower vases. If they slip a piece of waxed paper as a 'coaster' under the vase, there will be no marking problems."

COOL COMFORT

From a hot-weather hater: "Since a hot-water bottle is comforting, why not a **cold-water bottle**? I really suffer in hot weather, so I keep a hot-water bottle filled with water in my refrigerator during the daytime. By night it is well chilled but not iced. I take this to bed with me and it really does cool me off!"

SHAMPOO THOSE COLLARS!

From Connecticut: "I want to share my hint on how to clean the **collars** of work shirts and housedresses. Wet the shirt in warm water, then spread a line of liquid hair shampoo on the dingy circle on the collar.

"Drop the garment in your washing machine with hot or medium water and your regular soap. It's wonderful and will not fade colored shirts."

SEVEN RULES FOR WASHING CORDUROY

Here is the latest advice on how to keep **corduroy** as soft and velvety as when new:

1. Turn the garment inside out before washing. This will keep the lint from other clothes from adhering to the pile.
2. Use any mild soap and warm water. Squeeze suds through the fabric and rinse by pressing water out gently. *Never* twist or use a wringer on corduroy because this will set deep creases into the corduroy pile.
3. If you're using a washing machine, set at medium heat for water.
4. Use fabric softener in final rinse to restore velvety finish.
5. Hang up and allow to drip dry. If you use a drier, use it at medium heat and tumble the garment until nearly dry. Take out, shake off last drops and allow to drip dry.
6. Children's clothes done in this way often do not even require pressing.
7. For finest finish, press corduroy on the wrong side over a terry cloth towel. Use a steam iron and it will give a truly finished performance.

OFF THE CUFF

From Ohio: "I shine sterling silver **cuff links** with tooth paste when I am out of polish. It is very good."

Another way to shine up those silver **cuff links** is to rub them on a piece of wool clothing or carpet. In case you do not have carpets on your floor, men, turn up the cuff of your wool trousers. Rub the cuff links across the wool briskly four or five times. They will shine like new!

Did you know that dry baking soda will also clean sterling silver **cuff links?**

A NEW POINT OF VIEW

From Long Island: "I made some window **curtains** for our bathroom from striped bed sheets. To keep them from getting drenched each time we took a shower, I made an over-curtain of pure plastic to go across the entire window.

"The pretty striped curtains can be seen and kept dry at the same time."

From Omaha: "Know those plastic tablecloths we get on sale and use on our kitchen tables? Buy one and make a curtain for your bathroom out of it. These **curtains** are darling. The ruffles do not have to be hemmed and the plastic is very easy to sew. They may be removed from the window and rinsed in the bathtub, then put right back on the window. I bought a design that looked lacy and people have no idea it's a tablecloth."

CURTAIN TIME!

From Honolulu: "The yardstick is a convenience when hanging **curtains**. It is never easy to distribute the gathers at the top evenly. I spread them as evenly as possible, then step down off my ladder, get my yardstick and move my gathers into perfect folds. By standing away from the curtain and letting the yardstick do the work for you . . . it is easier to spot where too many folds are."

From Houston: "I have discovered a way to do my dacron crisscross picture-window **curtains** which makes them hang and drape like they did when they were new.

"This method requires no pre-starching. I wash and drip-dry them in the usual way. I hang them up and tie them back and drape the first curtain—getting all of the folds in perfect shape.

"Then I get out a can of spray starch and spray the curtain gently and let it dry. Later I do the top 'crossed' curtain in the same manner.

"Those curtains stay in place—just as you have draped them—until the next washing.

"If some of the starch goes through to the windowpane (this does happen if you get the spray can too close to the curtain), a bit of window cleaner on a cloth will take it off. Just reach up under the dry curtains and wipe it off. Or lay a newspaper against the pane before hanging the curtains and spraying with the starch, and remove it afterward."

From Cleveland: "I found that using thumb tacks on my tie-back **curtains** made an awful lot of holes in the window casings.

"I had my husband put the smallest size cup hooks on the edge of the casing, and then I made small button holes in my tie-backs. Any loop will do if you cannot make a button hole."

From Vermont: "I know people advise putting a knife in the end of a curtain rod to thread **curtains.** But I have found that I can clip off the finger of an old glove and place this on any rod in my house and it will allow the fabric to slide on the rod easily."

Another method for those who have trouble slipping the **curtain** rod through their curtains: Take the outside wrapper from a package of chewing gum and slip it over the curtain rod. The curtain will go through slick as a whistle.

From Florida: "The headings of my draw **curtains** began to droop and drop over so badly that I did not think I could use them any longer. It dawned on me that I could put cardboard in them and it perhaps would help. I cut lightweight cardboard the length and width of the pleats and took one or two pieces and tucked them up in each pleat. Now the folds look like new. No more drooping at all!"

From New Jersey: "Our dry-cleaning business is over a hundred years old. When we accept **curtains and draperies,** here is why we have to clean them 'at owner's risk':

"Many fabrics have white or very light backgrounds, which become yellow and streaky from sun, household smoking, furnace gasses and general exposure.

"If an afternoon's exposure on a sunny day at the beach can burn us, then what must happen to curtains and draperies hanging at windows for weeks and months?

"Curtains at windows which are never open can develop water marks—*cold* fabric condenses water just as glass panes do.

"Novelty fabrics, of course, are created solely for appearance and not for durability. Many 'wash and wear' fabrics stand up well if dipped in the tub every other week or two, but do not react as well when left hanging a year before being sent to the cleaner.

"The actual damage is done at the window and does not become apparent until the cleaning and finishing.

"Many of today's curtain and drapery fabrics do shrink, in spite of our best efforts to keep them to size, even with special stretching equipment. Why not be prepared for such shrinkage and have extra-wide hems, so that you or your decorator could let out the extra material when draperies are being cleaned?

"Examine your curtains and draperies carefully at least every other month. Dust them or vacuum them periodically. You may be surprised at their condition!"

From Denver: "I have pricked my fingers on **curtain** stretchers so many times that I no longer use them. When I wash a thin panel, whether starched or otherwise, I stretch a blanket on the carpet in the living room, place a bed sheet over it and get out my package of straight pins.

"I lay the thin panel down on the sheet and stick the pins into the blanket on the floor. This will hold beautifully and you will not hurt your fingers.

"Another good thing about this—you can use the edge of the sheet as a guide and your curtain will be perfectly straight. So no warped edges, the kind you get from ironing on an ironing board. If your curtain needs further starch, either make your own and put it in a spray bottle or use the prepared spray-type starch. This can be done beautifully while the curtain is on the floor, as the starch gets on evenly, plus the fact that any left over will hit the sheet, which can be washed later.

"Those who do not starch their curtains but find they get

a little dry while being stretched with this method, may put plain water in a plunger-type of bottle and dampen the curtains slightly. I found this to be the best method so far."

DRAPERY DO'S AND DONT'S

For those of you who have out-sized windows, such as picture windows, bedspreads are wonderful for making **draperies.** They are cheap, too.

They are no trouble at all to make. Just split the spread in half and hem the torn sides. Make a heading at the top to run your rods through. They may also be pinch-pleated, if you are so inclined. Bedspreads are especially good for draw draperies, as they do not have to be lined.

For older homes with long narrow windows, bedspreads can't be beaten for draperies and curtains. Watch for sales. Many stores put these spreads on sale when they get down to broken stock.

I suggest that you consider buying full-size bedspreads no matter what size your window is. These make the drape fuller and they are usually the same price . . . when on sale.

I bought the spreads with fringe around the edges. The fringe was left on the spreads and used on the inside and bottom of the curtain in place of the usual ruffle. Real cute.

I also would like to pass on another hint. When making these curtains, use a big stitch on your sewing machine. You will have no "pull" on a curtain as you ordinarily would in clothing. A big stitch goes faster and you can make a straighter seam and hem. I also suggest using mercerized thread when sewing on hobnail or chenille spreads.

And, gals, if you have maple or ranch-type furniture, try the white hobnail spreads. They are so colonial looking. Later, if you get tired of the white, which I did, throw the spreads in your washing machine and tint them! I tinted one set pale peach. The next year, when I got tired of peach, I just bleached them white again in my machine.

From Kansas City: "I have the simplest method of lining **draperies** that one could imagine and I think others would like it, too.

"Instead of lining the drapery itself and sewing in the lining, some people make two identical pieces, one lining and one outside drape. These are usually placed on two rods. My method even eliminates the second rod and the lining is easier to wash.

"My lining is made straight (with old sheets) and in a separate piece, just like a shower curtain! I hem the sides, top and bottom of the material, then put small buttonholes across the top. I use the buttonholes to slip over the drapery hooks on the inside of the drapery and sew small snaps at intervals along each side so the lining stays neatly in place.

"This lining is much easier to wash and iron than attached linings are. The inside straight 'sheet' may be sent to the laundry or done in your washing machine, and the drapery itself sent to the cleaners.

"I have used this method on both ready-made drapes and those I have made myself with pleater tape."

From Arizona: "The first time I washed my washable **draw draperies** I was disappointed in the results. They lost their stiffness at the top and the pleats dropped. I had better luck the second time, and here's how I did it:

"After washing them I rolled them in a big bath towel and let them sit for about ten minutes. I removed them from the towel and rehung them. Now, here is what does the trick . . .

"Draw the drapes *closed*. Pinch pleats together with your fingers, slip rust-proof bobby pins over the *top* of each pleat. Use rubber-tipped bobby pins to prevent any damage to the fabric. Make sure there is no rust on the pins, which could mark the drapes.

"While the drapes are still damp, spray them lightly and evenly with a spray starch starting at the top. When you have sprayed the complete drapery . . . spray across the top again! During the time the draperies are drying, run your hand down the edges, holding them between your thumb and forefinger, exerting slight pressure. This prevents puckering.

"When the draperies are completely dry, remove the bobby pins, spread them out, and the pleats are as good as new!"

From Louisiana: "Instead of buying custom-made **draperies** for my large picture windows, I bought two pairs of regular draperies and sewed them together."

From Rhode Island: "Aren't **draw draperies** beautiful? And aren't they expensive? But don't they make you mad when you are trying to open or close them and you can't find the right 'pull'? I have had draw draperies for years and used to get mad every time I tried to find the right string.

"Then it finally dawned on me! Mark one 'pull' string. How? Fingernail polish!

"I painted the little ball on the end of the string that opens the drapery with pink fingernail polish (my draperies are pink). More troubles! I couldn't tell which string to pull when they were open, because both cords lay on the floor. Then I thought of a better idea.

"When the drapes were closed, I painted exactly where my hand usually grabs the cord (I could tell, because the cord was dirty!). This solved my problem. Now, each morning when the curtains are closed, I will grab the 'pink place' in the cord and pull it open.

"Paint only the cord that opens the drapes. An unpainted cord will mean 'to close'."

Having trouble with traverse **drapery** rods not drawing easily? Open the drapery and rub the inside of the traverse thoroughly with common paraffin wax. It will scoot along like magic!

From Chicago: "Here is a hint for finding the right **drapery** cord to pull: I tie a big knot at the point at each end of the cord where my hand reaches behind the drapes to pull the proper cord.

"That way I do not have to look to see if I get the right pull . . . whether to open or close the draperies . . . the one with the knot is the correct one to pull. The other is at the top, out of reach."

From Los Angeles: "Why do **draperies** rot only on one side of the room? The rest of my draperies are perfectly good.

"Draperies and curtains should be interchanged . . . frequently. Remove the draperies and curtains from one window and put them on the other side of the room if at all possible. Exposure to the sunlight rots the drapery, especially if it comes through a windowpane. (Or take the drapery or curtain from the left-hand side of the window and hang it on the right-hand side.)

"By changing the draperies you are prolonging the life of the one which you have removed from the window. This way they will all 'give out' at the same time.

"When you do your spring and fall housecleaning, vacuum or put your draperies in your drier—without heat—and tumble them a while. This will remove most of the dust. And remember, draperies and curtains must be dry-cleaned or washed once in a while to prevent further rot and deterioration."

From Alabama: "I heard of washing fiber-glass **draperies** by hanging them on the clothesline and turning the garden hose on them. Well, I tried something else.

"I put some liquid detergent in a liquid sprayer, which we attached to our garden hose. I sprayed my drapes well with these mixed suds and then sprayed them again with clear water.

"I could actually see the spots coming clean as I sprayed my draperies while they were hanging on the line. It was a lot easier than using the bathtub to wash them. I am positive that I prevented wrinkles by using this method."

WHEN YOU GIVE A DARN

A hint from Illinois: "I have a new idea for **darning** husband's black socks that I think other women should know about. I use my husband's flashlight. The material in the socks is very dark. When your eyes are as old as mine, you can turn the flashlight on the exact spot you are sewing and it is a great help."

FIRST AID FOR DACRONS

From a Kentucky gentleman: "My **dacron** shirts have become quite discolored. I can pour almost straight bleach on them and they still aren't white. What do I do?"

First and foremost: Never wash dacron with colored fabrics! These man-made fabrics seem to absorb color from other materials. I don't care if it's a pale blue bath towel that has been washed 120 times, *don't* wash anything colored with white man-made fabrics.

Now that you have ruined your shirts, I suggest that you dissolve one cup of a *dishwashing machine compound* (be sure to follow the caution directions on the box) to one gallon of warm water in a *glass* or an *enameled* container. Put your discolored shirts in this solution.

Soak them at a temperature of about 130-140 degrees for thirty minutes to one hour. Or you can leave them overnight at room temperature. Then wash your articles as usual.

Be sure the dishwashing compound is *completely* dissolved before plunging in your discolored articles. I suggest that you use a "plumbers' friend" (this is the gadget used to unstop drain pipes) and massage the articles up and down for a while. This will save your hands.

Be sure to use a glass or enameled pan or pot—*not* aluminum.

This works on articles of 100 percent dacron and some types of dacron blends. After all, your garment is already discolored, so what do you have to lose now?

MULTIPLY DETERGENT SUPPLY

Here's how to save on liquid **detergent;** no matter what brand you use . . . it will go farther:

When that bottle you are using now is on its last dregs . . . don't throw the bottle away. Save it. When you open a new bottle, pour half of the liquid detergent in this "empty." Fill *both* with warm water. Shake well . . . and set aside.

See if your detergent doesn't last nearly twice as long! We often use too much soap and detergent, no matter where we use it. So give this idea a whirl.

Bet you will enjoy the crowd of savers (that's *us*) once you try it.

If you ever run out of liquid detergent, take some powdered detergent, mix it with warm water and let it set a while. It makes a liquid detergent. Much easier to squirt than pour . . .

LOOK, MA—NO HANDS!

This is how I do my **dishwashing:** I scrape them, rinse them under the cold-water faucet and stack them either in one side of the sink or on the drainboard.

I plug the sink up, pour in my detergent and turn on the hot-water faucet full blast. I use no cold water. First I put my silverware in, placing dishes on top of this, and glasses around the sides.

Then I forget them.

After the water is completely cold, and not before, I pull the plug from the sink and let the detergent water drain completely.

I turn on the hot-water faucet. (If you don't have one of those little dime-store spray gadgets that fit on your faucet, run to your nearest dime store and buy one.) I take a little vegetable brush and rinse the dishes and set them in my dish drainer to drain.

I never use the place in the dish drainer to drain silverware. I always stand my silver vertically in a jar. This prevents spotting because the water drains down and off the silver. I place silver with knife blades and fork tines up.

Some good points about this method are:

It saves your hands. They are not in the hot water. Neither are they in harsh detergents, which is bad for cuticles and fingernails.

You save time. You can save approximately fifteen minutes each dishwashing session if this method is used. Test it yourself. I did. This is also fifteen minutes you are not standing on your feet.

Naturally each pan has been washed as soon as the vegetables are emptied from it. Just use that little scrub brush, turn on that wonderful spray gadget and wash them while the food is still warm and soft. It's easier. Rinse under hot-water faucet and turn upside down to dry while you are eating dinner. Then all you have to do is put them away. Pots and pans are half the battle of a clean kitchen.

With the drainboard clean, your pans put away and your dishes under nice hot suds and water, that kitchen looks nice. So—no depression. At least I found it so.

These same dishes are usually the very ones you will use at the next meal. So why not just leave them in your drainer until you are ready to set the table again? If you are a real fanatic you can cover them with a clean dishcloth or piece of pretty plastic. I sometimes take the dish drainer to the dining-room table with all the dishes still in it! Set the table and empty the drainer in one procedure and all in one trip. Why waste time taking the dishes out of the drainer, the same dishes?

Clock yourself. See how many minutes it takes you to empty your dish drainer and put the dishes away. Then add the minutes it takes you to remove those same dishes from the cabinet again and set the table. Multiply this by the number of meals you expect to cook in a lifetime and glory be, you could take a vacation with the time you have saved!

RAGTIME!

From Rhode Island: "I have discovered that I can take my old discarded nylon curtains, stitch about eight thicknesses together on the sewing machine, and have the grandest **dishrag** ever! The best size is ten inches square. I make about five of them at the same time. They are wonderful—they never 'sour.'"

The **dishrags** we make from dime-store nylon net (less than forty cents a yard and seventy-two inches wide!) are wonderful for scrubbing pots and pans, taking baths, covering a bar of soap and a thousand other things, but . . . a new idea just hit me after a woman complained that they wouldn't pick up water spots on her Formica drainboard.

I took an old washrag, cut a piece of net to fit and stitched them together around the edges on my sewing machine.

If I want friction, I turn the net side down. If I want

absorption, I turn the cloth side down. Washes beautifully in the washing machine, too.

And just try these for taking a bath!

From Maryland: "For those who still use the old-fashioned **dishrags** . . . the very last thing I do at night in my kitchen is clean the sink with a cleanser that contains bleach. I do not rinse the dishrag, but leave it in a corner of the sink overnight. The next morning I rinse it and have a very bright, clean rag."

STEEL YOURSELF AGAINST THAT HOT SPOT!

I have found a good solution for those who have literally burned, baked, blistered and deep-rusted their Formica drainboards.

Here's the pitch: Why replace an expensive **drainboard** (and, gals, it is expensive . . . just call and price a replacement!) when you will most likely put down another hot pan in exactly the same place again? This is called perpetual replacement! I know!

Here's the answer: Go out and buy a piece of stainless steel (have the edges beveled if you want to) and place this over the burned spot. Have the man bore four little holes, one on each corner, and buy four screws to fit. Screw this "steel hot-board" over the burned spot and your troubles will be ended.

This hot-board can be used to place pans on, hot spoons on, cut lettuce, make sandwiches, etc. It's wonderful to cut vegetables and slice sandwiches on, as the stainless steel also keeps your Formica from getting cut up.

This method of covering up a spot will pay for itself in the long run. We always need some place to put that pot of potatoes while we are mashing them.

And for those of you who don't have a burned spot . . . it's a good idea to get the hot-board anyway, because if you get it before you burn your drainboard, then you can place it where you really want it.

Looks neat on your cabinet, too. Ends that worry about yelling at the family about not cutting the drainboard, or "don't set that hot pot on the drain—I've told you twenty times!"

I know, I know. That piece of steel was the best money I ever spent in the kitchen.

SCREEN TEST

From Maryland: "My suggestion for carefree **drains** is to cut a bit of window-screening to fit the top of your drainpipe and bind it with iron-on tape. Laid over the drain in the shower, tub or wash basin at shampoo time, this little piece of wire screening catches all the lint, loose hair, etc. Saves stopped-up drains and lots of plumbing bills. Try it!"

DRESS UP—AND DOWN

From Colorado: "Here is a nice way to lengthen a little girl's **dress** and give it a new look:

"Cut the dress off at the hem, then scallop the bottom of the dress. These may be large or small scallops, depending on the material in the dress. The scallops may be hemmed, or bound with braid or rickrack, lace, or even lined.

"To make small scallops, use a juice glass for a pattern and trace around it. For larger scallops, use the edge of a saucer. To get them even, use a strip of tape on the plate at the depth you want your scallops to be.

"Then add a flounce under the scallops for the needed length.

"The flounce may be cotton, nylon, silk, velvet, embroidery or lace. In fact, any material that will contrast with the dress.

"Oh . . . mothers who do not want to bother with scalloping can simply cord the bottom of the dress and then add the flounce."

From Denver: "An easy way to shorten an old **dress** with a full skirt which is cut on the bias is to cut it off to the desired length with pinking shears. Then sew narrow velvet ribbon on the edge. A belt of the same piece of velvet looks nice. I have done this twice, and the dresses have looked better than when they were new!"

When you're making a **dress** or skirt or even just making some alterations on a garment, instead of basting in seams or a hem, use ordinary hair clips! The broad, flat kind are wonderful for clipping along the side seams and are just fabulous for holding hems in dresses!

All you have to do is simply measure the hem, slide on the hair clips, and then when you're stitching in place, either by machine or by hand, just slide the clips off as you go along.

NEW LOOK FOR AN OLD DRIVEWAY

To cover an old black asphalt **driveway,** this is what we did at our home:

We wet the driveway thoroughly with water from the garden hose, leaving a thin sheet of water on the asphalt. We took one bag of cement and sprinkled it by handfuls in circles on the asphalt, being sure not to cover more than three feet of space at any one time.

With an old kitchen broom, we "swept" the cement in circles over the asphalt until the entire driveway was covered. The cement sank into the little holes in the asphalt and completely covered our old, ugly driveway.

We found two things were necessary. Don't drive your car on the fresh cement for a few days until it is completely dry, and never let the fresh concrete dry too fast. We sprinkled our driveway about twice a day with the fine spray of the garden hose to keep it moist and allow for slow drying.

And, gals, if you try to do this yourself, use an old broom and be sure to wash it after use (before the cement hardens on the bristles). But I suggest that you do this on a weekend when your husband is there to help you. (Compliment *him* when he is doing this to give him inspiration to complete the job. It works. I know!)

A WATCHED POT . . .

From Vermont: "When I make drop **dumplings** in broth, I put an inverted glass pie plate on top of the kettle as a lid. This way I can see when my dumplings are done without lifting the lid and letting the steam escape!"

AS EASY AS CHILD'S PLAY

From a grateful reader: "You taught me the convenience of using a child's broom for some chores, so I also bought a child's mop. I have found wonderful uses for it.

"I am seventy and can't reach very high, nor do I bend easily. I use the little mop (dry) to reach over the windows and dust high places. I wash it often.

"I bought another one to use on the kitchen floor. I also use the mop for waxing. No bending when it comes to washing it, either."

DUSTING MITTEN

Grandma says: "I put a plastic bag as a mitten over my hand *before* dusting my furniture. Now, no more oily hands for me.

"My dusting rag is then put away in the same plastic mitten by turning the plastic bag wrong side out and leaving the rag in it."

FOR THAT SHOWER OF DUST

From New York: "For those whose home accumulates a great deal of dust and lint . . . listen to the way I solved the back-breaking problem of cleaning under my bed.

"I had an old shower curtain. I opened it flat and stretched it out under the bed. All of the dust and lint from my chenille bedspreads, cotton carpets and so forth end up on this old shower curtain instead of embedding itself in my carpets.

"About once a week I pull the shower curtain out from under the bed, fold it carefully, take it outside and shake it. That's all! This saves me the back-breaking job of moving the bed and sweeping under it weekly. The shower curtain does not show because the bedspread hides it!"

WHEN YOU'RE HAVING A SHELL OF A TIME . . .

From Oklahoma: "Here's a tip for getting a piece of egg shell out of an egg that has been broken into a dish. Instead of trying to fish it out with a spoon or your fingers, take half of the empty egg shell and scoop it out. It comes out on the first try!"

From New Mexico: "The cleverist thing I know: When I boil eggs and put them in the refrigerator and can't tell if they are hard boiled or not, I spin the eggs.

"If they spin and go 'round and 'round, they're hard boiled. If they wobble and don't spin, they're raw."

. . . BE DEVILISH

From New Hampshire: "When I fix deviled eggs I cut them in half crosswise and remove the yolk.

"Then I cut a bit of the rounded point off the bottom of the eggs. This way the eggs stand up wherever you put them and it solves the problems of the egg turning-over if you do not happen to have a special dish for that purpose."

And while you are at it, my dear, may I tell you not to waste the little pieces of white you have cut off? Put these in with the yolks and mash them all at the same time. This gives you more yellow to fill out the center of your eggs.

Sometimes when I am deviling a dozen eggs for a picnic, let's say, if I happen to have any torn whites I also put these in with the yolks.

If I am having a party and deviling lots of eggs, I always

add extra whites anyway so that I will have lots of filling to heap in the center of the egg.

Another little hint is to sprinkle the deviled eggs with a dash of paprika. Paprika is inexpensive and lends color to that homemade deviled egg and makes it look like those fancy restaurant eye-catchers.

HOME REPAIR . . . ON THE RANGE

From Carmel: "I have an **electric range.** It is the kind that has oodles of buttons on it. The last time one button went 'kaflooey,' I had to call a repairman. You wouldn't believe the charge!

"I asked him just what caused the damage. Do you know what he told me? He said it was everyday use: grease spatters, etc., that had gotten down into the buttons and had messed up the mechanism.

"Now I tear off a little piece of plastic wrap and cover all the buttons with one piece of plastic wrap!

"This keeps the grease, the heat and the vapors from the house and kitchen from getting down into those little buttons.

"You do not need to remove the plastic to operate the buttons. And you can take a sponge and either wipe off the grease spatters and accumulated dust from the top of this plastic, or replace it with some new plastic."

Thanks! I'm sure you'll save lots of repair bills for us women who have electric ranges. Bless you.

CURRENT COMFORT

From Rhode Island: "I have found that by using a sheet blanket over my **electric blanket** it isn't necessary to launder the electric blanket for many months. Pull the sheet blanket to the top and then turn it back over the electric blanket about six inches. The blanket retains the heat longer, too, and it isn't necessary to turn the heat up so far."

WHEN IT'S A SHOCKING MATTER

From Missouri: "Bothered with static **electricity** when you touch doorknobs on a cold day? I use those little knitted stretch covers (for the bottoms of glasses or soda pop bottles) on my metal doorknobs. They really do the trick. Fold one in half and slip it over the doorknob. It's great!"

From New York: "Tell us what to do about static **electricity** in our homes. I am tired of being shocked each time I touch the light switch. Yes, I do have wall-to-wall carpeting."

I am told by big carpet manufacturers that static electricity is caused from dry atmosphere. By introducing moisture into the room, most of the "shocks" are eliminated.

If you remember back in the old days of radiators, wood stoves and flat-top kitchen stoves, you used to see Mama and Papa set a pan of water on top of it for what is called surface evaporation. A tea kettle on the kitchen stove does a pretty good job because it is putting moisture into the air, too.

However, we burn a 24-hour vaporizer in our home—yep, the kind a child uses when he has the croup—during all of the cold months when the heat is on.

Another thing . . . on the days when it rains, raise some of your windows a bit and let the moisture in the air come into your home. Especially when it is foggy outside. Fog is a wonderful "vaporizer." Full of moisture!

There are also all kinds of static electricity preventive products on the market. But the National Institute of Rug Cleaning says: "Some chemicals you might apply directly on your rug could cause more rapid re-soiling. If you can just raise the humidity in your home you are far better off."

The strangest thing of all . . . have you ever noticed that when you walk around the house barefoot, stocking-footed, or in knitted-type booties you never get static electricity or a shock?

Here's a way to test it in your home:

Dragging your feet, walk across your carpeted room or down a hall. Then touch a metal object. Do this while bare-footed and then try it again while wearing your leather-soled shoes. You will be knocked for a flip!

DON'T BE SHOCKING!

If you are planning to wear a certain type of dress that causes static **electricity,** hang it in the bathroom while you're taking a hot shower. This allows the steam to get into the material and thus prevents static electricity. This works well for men's suits, too.

RE-ELASTIC

Here's one: Whenever **elastic** that is sewed to a garment becomes worn out or stretched . . . just baste cord elastic through the worn-out elastic. Pull it up and knot it.

This is fine for half-slips, underpants, pajamas and all children's garments. Yes, even hubby's shorts!

Sometimes it is difficult to find a needle with an eye large enough to do this by hand, but you can do it by getting a "crewel" needle.

Cord elastic can be found in dime stores.

EYELIGHTS

To get a sharp point on your mechanical **eyebrow pencil,** take a piece of fine sandpaper and keep it handy in your medicine cabinet.

Each time you use the pencil, just hold the pencil at an angle and draw across the rough sandpaper. Rub it around gently and you will get a beautiful new point. It is like using a new eyebrow pencil each time.

Those of you ladies who wear bifocals . . . use them when you pluck your **eyebrows.** Those who do not wear them will never know what a help this is.

Just turn your glasses upside down and set them a little bit further down on your nose and pluck away. This is also good when you're lining eyebrows with a pencil. . . .

STRAIGHT FROM THE HEARTH

I'd like to pass on a few ideas about **fireplaces.** Most people start fire in a wood-burning fireplace with newspapers. Even if you don't, the fireplace will still end up with ashes and debris, and with most fireplaces, it eventually *must* be removed! This is the job most people hate. I did, too, until I learned a little secret recently.

Take a cardboard box and place it on your hearth when it comes cleaning time. Then get out that old shovel. Take your sprinkler—the gadget you sprinkle clothes with—and *gently sprinkle* the ashes *before* pushing the shovel underneath the debris.

Now, if you do not have a sprinkler you can take a pan of water, dip your fingers in it, and lightly sprinkle the charred residue just as our grandmothers sprinkled clothes before the fancy sprinkler gadgets came into existence!

Wet only the *top* of the pile of debris. This will settle the dust particles and bits of charred paper before you pick up the mess. Caution: don't use too much water because you do not want it running out over your hearth. After you have done this once and dipped up one shovelful into the box, you will know exactly how much water to apply. All you want to do is wet the top.

And before I forget, it is really neater to open up a newspaper and line the cardboard box with it. Leave the paper sticking up about eight or ten inches on the sides of the box itself. This way you can—after putting the debris into the box—fold the top of the newspaper over and thus eliminate any flying particles when you carry it through the house.

I know fireplaces are messy, but aren't they just wonderful?

From Tennessee: "After seven years with a commercial and residential cleaning firm in our city, I believe I have the solution to smoked **fireplaces:**

"Most stores handle art gum erasers. Buy yourself a couple of these and just start erasing . . . they work especially well on porous, rock-front fireplaces.

"On *smooth* stone or brick, wash with a strong solution of trisodium phosphate (one-half cup to one gallon of water). Use this with a sponge and use it only *after* all smoke possible has been erased with your art gum eraser."

From Pennsylvania: "I have found that vinegar will clean the brick tiling around my **fireplace.** I dip a vegetable brush in plain yellow vinegar and scrub the fireplace quickly with it. Then I take a sponge and absorb the moisture. Just look and see how dirty your sponge is! Of course, for very dirty fireplaces this may have to be repeated."

I clean **fireplace** hearth tiles and slate with a cream made of soft soap and skimmed milk. This really makes dark green slate look especially good.

As I told this to my husband he got up from his chair and made some of the mixture. He polished the slate entry that is in front of the fireplace. The slate looked just as though it had been waxed!

MAKE ARTIFICIAL FLOWERS BLOOM AGAIN

From Kentucky: "Before discarding artificial **flowers** that have become soiled, try this. Pour a cupful of salt into a large paper bag. Put a few flowers at a time into the bag and shake vigorously. The salt probably won't look soiled to you at first, but wait until you see the color of it when you pour it into the sink and turn the water on. I think you will be amazed!"

From Montreal: "I have some plastic **flowers** which are set in a plastic container. I dusted and cleaned them with a small cloth, but they still looked dull until I found out that I could put a drop or so of liquid detergent in each flower and set the whole thing in the bathtub and turn the shower on full force. They wash and rinse themselves."

From Nevada: "For those who have plastic or wax **flowers** in their home—if you grow tired of the color or the flowers have become faded or dirty, here's an idea. I wash mine and place them on the kitchen windowsill to dry.

"Then I take a bottle of fingernail polish (sometimes pink and sometimes bright red) and paint the flowers again. I find that the polish withstands many washings—and even sunlight and rain . . . just in case you are like me and put them in your flower beds sometimes. Yes, I do that!"

Another idea for plastic **flowers** that fade: Just get a can of spray paint and spray away! This is especially good when you get tired of pink roses and want some yellow or silver ones and the budget doesn't allow for them.

WHEN YOU'RE IN A FRAMING FRAME OF MIND

Here is a hint for tired picture **frames:**
Sand the frames with very fine sandpaper until they are satin smooth. Then use ordinary sewing-machine oil to get that beautiful, hand-rubbed finish. No varnish, shellac or wax is necessary.
This also works on unfinished new frames.

From Connecticut: "For those who buy unfinished picture **frames**—I have learned that they may be stained beautifully with just about anything.

"I am an artist and the best thing I've found, especially if you want the old-type 'mildew-and-mold' finish, is to buy some chalk at your dime store. Go over the frame thoroughly. This cheap, white chalk fills up the pores.

"Then, take a powder puff and dip it into any can of paste-type *shoe* polish (if your furniture is black use black, if your furniture is mahogany use red-type, if it's brown use regular brown polish, etc.) and smear it over the picture frame. Be sure to get it very thick in the corners.

"Take a piece of paper toweling, tissue or whatever you happen to have, place on soiled side of puff and turn the powder puff over. Use this to buff the frame thoroughly.

"You will get a sheen on the frame that is amazing! The chalk—which has gotten into the pores of the wood—will provide that old antique look."

FOR POP-FREE FRYING

From an elderly lady: "People should know that a colander can be inverted over a skillet when **frying** anything where grease is popping (bacon, chicken, etc.). Heat escapes but spatters are caught on the colander. Saves cleaning the stove."

FRUIT OF THE WEEK

From a disposal owner: "Once a week I cut up a citrus **fruit** such as a lime or lemon (or better yet, use the skin of a grapefruit) and run this through the disposal. A sweet and fresh smell is the result."

SEEING IS BELIEVING

From New York: "I find metal canisters are for the birds. I can't see how much flour is left. I keep my **flour** in apothecary bottles. These bottles have a large mouth and I can see what I have. And no 'snow' job when you try to refold the paper flour sack!

"Apothecary jars are nice looking on the kitchen cabinet, too . . . give the look of distinction."

MUSEUM PIECE OF ADVICE

From the director of a museum: "Here is the recipe for the **furniture polish** we use in the museum. It is wonderful.

"Use: *One-third cup of each:* boiled linseed oil, turpentine, vinegar.

"Mix together and shake well. Apply with soft cloth and wipe completely dry with another clean soft cloth afterward.

"Don't try to boil your own linseed oil . . . it is *not* the same! Buy it at paint or hardware stores."

g

A HINT OF GARLIC

A happy homemaker writes: "For those who like **garlic** flavor, but not the full taste of the bud, I keep a sliced clove of garlic in a separate bottle of vinegar to use only for making salad dressing and the like.

"After a while, I have a delightful homemade garlic vinegar."

Here's a similar answer from a man who sympathizes with people who can't take the real **garlic** bud bite in salad dressing.

Pour some cider vinegar in a bottle, add your oil and spices, celery salt, etc. Cut those garlic buds in little pieces and put them in your bottle of oil and vinegar. Let this sit as long as you want to. The longer the better! The flavor will be absorbed by the oil.

I found that if the dressing is put in a bottle that has a plastic top with holes, it will keep the pieces of garlic buds from getting directly on the salad. Besides, the holes give one a more "sprinkled" area on a tossed salad.

A GRATER IDEA

Comments from a keen cook: "Instead of cutting or dicing cheese when I make scalloped potatoes or cheese and macaroni . . . I use my vegetable **grater.**

"I chill the cheese a little first, in the top part of my refrigerator. Then, with the grater, you will get thin, little curls that will melt immediately and mix better."

From a former finger-grater: "After fifteen years of grating carrots and cabbage for salads on my dime-store grater and grating my fingernails or fingers along with them many times, my husband came up with the idea that I use two thimbles on my fingers. No more grated nails!"

GRAVY—SMOOTH AS SILK

From Montreal: "For a quick and lumpless **gravy** I keep a jar filled with a mixture of half *cornstarch* and half flour. I put three or four tablespoonfuls of this mixture in another jar and add some water. In a few seconds I have a smooth paste for all of my gravy."

GRAVY TIP

A **gravy** hint from a reader: "For those who really want to save and make good gravy, too . . . try using powdered milk!

"As long as you are mixing your flour with water in a fruit jar, put the powdered milk in at the same time. By shaking the jar (or stirring it with an iced-tea spoon or long fork) you have completed two operations with one procedure. Pour into the drippings and—voilà!"

WHILE THEY SIZZLE

From a Sunday pancake-maker: "When cooking **griddle cakes,** I put a pat of butter on each griddle cake after I turn it over in the pan to cook the other side.

"How I wish they would do this in restaurants! They wait until they have all orders ready before serving and more often than not the pancakes are too cool to melt the butter by the time they are served!"

TEN PINS, ANYONE?

When you buy detergents and bleaches in large plastic bottles . . . don't throw the empties away. Use them to make a **game** of "ten pins" for your children. Partially fill each jug with sand or water and replace the cap. Set them in the usual manner and use a large rubber ball to knock them over!

Children can play this game in the driveway. Put chalk marks where each pin sets and for the foul line. It's a new game to them and costs nothing out of the budget.

SAVE . . . THEN THROW AWAY!

From a Dallas reader: "Save the cardboard from laundered shirts. It is ideal for the bottom of grocery sacks . . . converts them into reinforced **garbage** sacks!"

GIFT OF LOVE

Here is a little **gift** trick for anyone who likes to sew and is faced with the problem of what to give at that next baby shower.

Buy a yard and a quarter of corduroy and some matching blanket binding. Sew the binding around the edge of the corduroy either by hand with a pretty stitch or by machine. The results are just lovely, inexpensive, and the best receiving blanket ever made.

This blanket will be larger than the "store bought" kind, lint free and will wash beautifully in the washing machine.

Lucky Mother will never stop singing your praises for such a practical gift. These aren't bought in stores!

IN A PINCH

For those of you who have gained a few pounds lately and wear a **girdle** with "stays" . . . any time a stay jabs you in the flesh, take a piece of moleskin foot plaster and stick a little piece of it at the point where the stay jabs. This will bring enough comfort so that you can get by for a while. This also works on bras, especially the strapless type where the stays hurt. Now don't laugh, try it first!

NAME-DROPPERS

From Michigan: "When I entertain guests, I mark the water glasses with each person's name with nailpolish. While they're still wet, I sprinkle them with the metallic flakes that beauty shops use at New Year's time for hair. The flakes come in small vials with screw caps and perforated tops which make them easy to use.

"This method of marking saves using placecards, and you never give anyone the wrong glass. The names can be removed with nailpolish remover later!"

RELEASE THE GREASE

From New York: "I use my husband's aerosol can of shaving cream to remove **grease** from my hands. It leaves a nice smell, too. Just rinse with warm water and that's it."

From Iowa: "Mix a few grains of sugar with soap lather to remove **grease** and grime from the hands."

HAND-IN-GLOVE

From Delaware: "I have found the secret of keeping white cotton **gloves** white!

"I am an executive businesswoman and must wear white gloves every day. And they must be immaculate every time I shake hands with someone.

"The real secret is: After they are thoroughly washed and you are sure the fibers are *well* soaked with water and soap has been *well* rinsed out, use a little starch in your final rinse water.

"The starch not only brings new life into the glove but— from the next person who shakes hands with you, the next doorknob you open, the next satchel you carry or baby carriage you push—the glove will not absorb the soil as fast as it would if not starched. The starch prevents dirt from being absorbed into the tissues of the fabric itself."

From Honolulu: "I would like to tell our friends who wear kid **gloves** and like them clean that I use an art gum eraser! I just put the gloves on my hands, pick up the art gum eraser and rub. The gloves are cleaned in a jiffy. It will work on any color without harm. Just be sure your eraser is clean, gals."

From Washington, D.C.: "The trick to mending rubber **gloves** is to mend them *before* they need it! And while they are still brand new!

"Turn gloves inside out. Put a thimble on the finger that you are working on. Cut pieces of tape (I use adhesive) about a half-inch long. Make a little snip in the center of the tape on each side so the tape will overlap smoothly.

"Put these strips of tape on the tip of each finger (your thimble will keep it from flattening), and your gloves are ready to use! This tape won't make the fingers bulky."

DON'T BE STUCK UP!

A lady from Monterey writes: "I ruined about five pairs of rubber **gloves** because they stuck together. It finally dawned on me that if I put talcum powder on my hands before putting on my gloves, it not only kept the gloves from sticking, but it made them go on easier!"

STOP GROUCHING ABOUT GROUT MESS!

From Miami: "I have such a mess around the **grout** in my bathroom where the tile wall touches the tub. I am disgusted, ashamed, and embarrassed every time a guest comes into the bathroom. How can I get rid of this mildew that accumulates on the filler between the bathtub and the tile?"

Don't be ashamed! Let me tell you what I have done, and it works perfectly. Take an old plastic squirt bottle and fill it with household bleach—I use the type of bottle we ordinarily pour our mustard and catsup into—and *squirt* this around the grout and let it set overnight. The next morning, all of the mildew will be gone! Try it. You don't have anything to lose except about two cents worth of bleach.

For rust stains on the **grout** between tiles in the bathroom, use a liquid rust remover on the stains and they will disappear like magic. After application, rinse with a mild solution of vinegar and water.

From Tennessee: "When going over the **grout** on the bathroom tile, I used white shoe polish and cut down the time by using the white polish in a plastic bottle with a tip applicator.

"Just wash the tile, let it dry and apply the shoe polish in all of the cracks. Allow to dry thoroughly and wipe off excess on the edges of the tile with a well wrung-out sponge, or buff with a soft clean sponge or cloth. You'll think you've just moved in!"

From California: "A white fingernail pencil is excellent for touching up the discolored **grouting** between tiles in the bathroom. I just moisten it and mark."

HAIR DO'S

From Oregon: "I do not happen to be fortunate enough to own a hair dryer, but I do have a makeshift one.

"When I am in a rush to get my **hair** set and dried, I remove the bag from my vacuum cleaner, turn the hose around to 'blow' and turn it on. Let it blow a second to remove any remaining dust.

"Then I set my hair while the motor is getting warm. I then wrap my head in a heavy bath towel, stick the end of the hose in my bath-towel turban and settle down for about twenty minutes. It works wonders in an emergency."

From Boston: "When I wash my **hair**, I put cold cream on my eyelids, eyebrows and face. This keeps the soap out of my eyes because the soap will detour."

These big **hairpins** (ordinarily used for long hair) are wonderful to hold those big brush hair rollers in place. Try it.

From Texas: "For the times I must roll my **hair** and get it dried quickly . . . I put water into a spray bottle and spray my hair gently after it is rolled on curlers, thus allowing for quick drying."

For a quick-drying **hair-set,** I put my curlers in a bowl of hot water. Drain the water, leaving the curlers in the bowl. Shake each curler as it is used and then roll hair. Cover the hair after it is rolled up with a *damp* hairnet. Just enough moisture for curls, but they will dry in a jiffy.

For a real quickie—just roll your hair with completely dry curlers and then cover the head tightly with a damp hairnet.

From Virginia: "Before I cut my **hair,** I put it up as usual. When it is dry I snip each curl off as I take the pins and rollers out. This way I never lose my place when I get to the back and I find it much easier to have any part of my hair the exact length I want it."

Here is a way to keep lint from forming on your **hair-brush:** put the thin part of a nylon stocking over the brush before brushing your hair. Then brush.

When the stocking is removed . . . all the loose hair and lint are caught in the stocking mesh, leaving a clean brush. These "stocking brush-catchers" can be made by cutting sections from the leg of a discarded stocking about the length of the brush itself.

For people who use color rinses on their **hair** and have no rubber gloves: I protect my hands from the dye by using two plastic bags!

Your hands will work freely inside the bags while you are applying the color rinse. When you are through you can throw the bags away. Result: no dyed hands.

HAPPY HOBGOBLINS

And from a Dallas mother: "This year why not make your children's **Halloween** costumes? It's easy and fun. Your children will love them, especially if you let them help.

"Little girls love to dress up as gypsies. Nothing could be simpler than creating a gypsy costume.

"A cast-off skirt of yours and a white blouse are the basis. For a sash you will need a wide strip of material long enough to knot around the waist and leave fairly long ends. Don't bother hemming this sash. Just cut it, or pink it if you have pinking shears.

"All gypsies must have jewelry and lots of it. Raid your jewelry box for old necklaces. If you can't find enough jewelry, buy a box of macaroni. Let your child paint the hard uncooked circles with tempera, then string them into loops of beads. If you happen to have a can of gold spray paint, lay the macaroni on newspapers and spray it gold.

"For earrings, take large brass curtain rings and tie circles of string to them. The strings are then looped around the child's ears!

"The finishing touches are a scarf around the head, and for this one night, let the child use real, honest-to-goodness make-up.

"Speaking of make-up, lots of little girls are thrilled just to go decked out as their mothers! This means letting them go all the way, with your discarded dresses, shoes, hats, bags and, of course, the make-up.

"A one-night stand as 'One-Eyed Dick' or 'Peg-Leg Pete' may interest your boys. The first item of a pirate costume is an old pair of jeans or pants. Cut the pants off about six inches from the bottom, then use scissors and slash a two-inch fringe around the cut edges.

"Next add an old black shirt, slash at the sleeves, and a scarf or bandana for his head.

"Sashes and brass curtain-ring earrings are used for this as for the gypsies. A dime-store rubber knife and an eye patch will complete this costume. To make the eye patch, cut a two-inch circle from black construction paper, punch holes on two sides, and pull a string through the holes and tie on the back of the head. There you will have as fine a pirate as ever walked the plank!

"Children's sleepers with attached feet may be transformed into many costumes with just a few extras. For instance, add long floppy ears made of soft fabric, a cotton fluff for a tail, a bunny mask, and you have 'Peter Rabbit' or 'Bugs Bunny.'

"Red sleepers become a devil costume with the addition of a red hood and a long tail. The tail may be made by sewing a tube of red cloth and stuffing it with paper.

"Use an old shirt to make a jerkin to wear over the sleepers, make a ruffle collar, a pointed hat, large pompon buttons, and you have a clown!

"When Halloween comes around, see what fun it can be. This year let's use our heads instead of our pocketbooks."

TRY A FOIL-BURGER

From Pennsylvania: "Campers and picnickers might like our suggestion for making **hamburger** patties.

"I wrap them in foil and put them in the freezer. When

I collect the food for our outing, I put them in an ice-cream bag.

"By the time we get to the camp and the fire is lit they are all thawed and ready to pop on the wire grill and are done in a jiffy.

"I season them with salt and pepper, etc., before wrapping them in the foil. I do not remove the foil when cooking. All of the juices stay inside and they never get burned this way."

BONED HAM

From Georgia: "When buying a picnic **ham,** have the butcher cut it lengthwise (through the flat side) into two pieces . . . like cutting a hot dog bun in two. Only cut all the way through the ham so that it will make two pieces.

"When the ham is cooked, the bone will *literally fall out* and leave the meat ready for perfect slicing."

"I found this out accidentally when I rented a furnished apartment for the season and there was not a large enough kettle or roasting pan to cook a picnic ham.

"The butcher said it was the first time he had ever had a request to cut a ham cross-fashion and that he would have his wife try it . . . sounded wonderful to him. We all know it is hard to slice around the bone if it is left in the ham."

STOCKING STUFF

To check an immediate run in nylon **hose,** did you know that you could use colorless nail polish? Of course, if that isn't on hand and the run is above the knee or someplace it does not show, red is always acceptable in an emergency. At least it keeps the run from running down to your ankle!

Sometimes we get down to our last pair of **hose.** Did you know that you could take off your stockings, wash them and rinse them, shake them very hard while holding them about midway where the knee area is, then all you have to do is put them in a bath towel and rub as if you were polishing a table? These nylons can be put back on immediately. After this is done, walk around for a few minutes before putting on your shoes.

When fastening seamed **hose** to garters, if you hook the back garters first, the seam will invariably be straight.

Some garters can be detached and worn reversed on your **hose** so that the "button" won't show through your skirt. Two-way-stretch girdles can be worn wrong side out if the garters are not detachable.

From Virginia: "I love the idea of tying a pair of **hose** together in a knot when removing them so I know which ones are mates, but I have learned a new way to knot my hose to identify them as 'everyday,' etc.

"I tie a loose knot in the foot of my everyday hose when I remove them and before I wash them. Then, as I pick up a pair of hose to put on, if they have a knot in the foot, I know they are everyday hose.

"Rolled hose in my drawer means it's a good pair but inside the rolled hose they're still knotted at the knee so the different brands and pairs do not get mixed. I never 'un-knot' nylon **hose** to wash or dry them.

AN ICE CAPADE FOR YOUR TABLE

From Ohio: "Have you ever made an **ice mold** as a cold harbor for foods that have to remain on the table for a while?

"Fill a large ring mold or an angel food pan with a border of small multicolored flowers and alternate with small shiny green leaves from bushes. Fill with water to the top of the pan and freeze several days before using.

"Unmold ice on a large pizza pan covered with foil, or on a large glass plate or silver tray.

"Around the edge of the ice mold, place a border of small green leaves. Place tiny gherkins, radish roses, stuffed olives and cherry tomatoes on the border of leaves. Fill the center of the mold with prepared sea food. It has a very colorful effect.

"You can vary the mold by filling the center with balls of watermelon, honeydew, cantaloupe and other diced fruits, using colored toothpicks for pickups."

I just took my angel food pan and tried this by using tiny ivy leaves and red cherries. I added six or so drops of green food coloring to the water before I poured it in. Exquisite!

I filled the pan halfway up with water, as I did not want my mold too deep.

After removing it from the freezer, I let it sit on the drainboard a while until I could spin it around with my finger. Then I turned this over on a bed of green lettuce leaves. I cut all of my tomato wedges, pickles, sliced canned pineapple, cherries and shrimp pieces on the lettuce around the outside of the mold.

I lined the *inside* of the center ring (that's the hole in the middle, gals) with *foil*. Into this little foil cup I put my shrimp sauce! The lining is needed to keep the sauce from becoming watery.

It was a knock-out at my party. Try it. You don't have to buy it. Just make it!

NO MORE STICKING

From a reader in San Diego: "Place a rubber fruit-jar ring under your **ice tray,** and the tray will not stick to the bottom of the freezer compartment."

MAKE YOUR OWN ICER

Teen-age parties require plenty of **iced drinks.** Here's a simple solution for icing these drinks: use your washing machine! If you have a top-loading washer, fill it with about six inches of cold water, pour in part of the ice, load it with bottled drinks and cover with more ice. They chill quickly. No bottles filling up a refrigerator, either.

Caution: Disconnect the washer while the party is in progress!

The next morning all you have to do is spin the water out of the machine. No mess, no toting of water, and a neat area after the party.

DICED ICE

A gentleman writes: "Instead of storing **ice cubes** in plastic bags and putting them in the refrigerator, crush the ice first and then store it in plastic bags. You can get more ice in your refrigerator per inch of space!

"Now, this ice might be slightly stuck together on removal, but so were the cubes I used to use! The plastic bag may be struck against any hard surface, and immediately all the ice comes loose."

PUT LAZY SUSAN TO WORK

From Wisconsin: "When there's **illness** in the house, it's a grand idea to drag out that Lazy Susan and put it on the bedside table.

"Put the medicine bottles and pills in the middle of the Lazy Susan with a glass of water.

"In each individual section, put all the little things the patient is likely to need, such as cough medicine and drops, medicine spoons, facial tissues, etc. Then, when the bed patient needs something, it saves you many steps . . . he can just rotate 'Susan.' Also it prevents cluttering up the bedside table.

"I always put an alarm clock in the middle of the gadget and set the alarm—when it goes off the patient knows it's time to take medicine."

When a child is **ill** . . . serve his food in a muffin tin. The cups can hold assorted foods. Even a small glass of milk can be set in one and prevent spills on a slippery bed tray. If one compartment is unused, float a flower in it.

I'M INCENSED!

Letter of laughter: "What is your one expensive luxury? Surely you have something that you indulge in which is above and beyond the necessities of life. Won't you share this with your neighbors?"

Yes, I do have one luxury. It's **incense!**

Having lived in China and Japan, I find that the few cents I spend for incense result in something most uplifting and inspiring. I don't know what it does, but no matter how poor the Chinese or Japanese are, they always burn incense.

After my family goes off to work and school, and before I get down to work, I light two cubes of incense. I place one in the living room and one in the back part of my house in an ash tray. The odor is so uplifting that it gives me inspiration to keep going because I know my house must be worthy. And it makes me feel like a lady!

Incense may be bought for from fifteen to twenty cents at the dime store. I figure it costs me less than a half-cent to burn a piece! So why not?

IDENTIFY THE BOOTS

Use a cotton swab dipped in household bleach to mark the children's **initials** on the inside of their galoshes and boots. The bleach will remove the color inside of the boot and the initials will clearly proclaim the owner.

ERASE THOSE INK SPOTS

From Vermont: "How can I remove ball point **ink** from my plastic upholstery? These little kiddies just will use ball point pens! I'm desperate; I've tried everything and cannot remove it."

It is my belief that ball point inks vary. Get to it as quickly as possible for best removal.

Sometimes cuticle remover will make the spot disappear. I dip an old terry cloth washrag in some cuticle remover and rub the spot. Other times rubbing alcohol will do the same job. However, I have had so many complaints that neither of these will work on certain kinds of materials that I have written to a plastics manufacturer. Here is his answer:

"Plastic upholstery is made to withstand scuffing, cracking, peeling and hard use. It will come up fresh and sparkling after a mild soap-and-warm-water cleaning followed by a clear-water rinse. Be sure to wipe dry. However, certain stains, if allowed to remain, become set and make removal more difficult. *It is important to remove these stains immediately.*

"If the plastic should get ball point ink on it, the stain should be removed immediately. Place a thin cotton pad over the stained portion and pour sufficient household bleach to wet the pad. Lift the pad at one-minute intervals and note if the stain has been removed. Do not prolong this contact. When the stain has been satisfactorily bleached, wash the area with a 3 percent solution of hydrogen peroxide, followed by a mild soap and water rinse."

WHEN THE NATIVES ARE RESTLESS . . . !

From Long Island: "Like all mothers, I dreaded the day when our **infant** baby wouldn't be content to stay in her playpen.

"We learned two tricks that I'd like to pass along: 1. An

old-fashioned triple mirror fastened securely in the corner of the playpen . . . baby played with the reflections for hours and loved it. 2. A little padded stool . . . only four inches high. We made it the length of the playpen, about eighteen inches wide.

"This was very adventurous for a child who didn't walk alone. It taught her to step up and down (she had the railing to hang onto), and at some times it was much fun for her just to kneel beside the stool or lie down on it."

From New Hampshire: "My **infant** son is fourteen months old. He is at the point where he would much rather be in my scrub pail than in his playpen.

"I just discovered that if I put all of his toys in a large paper bag, he will be happy pulling them out for at least a half hour longer than usual.

"I put the toys in the paper bag in his playpen after he has gone to bed. When he wakes up that bag is very intriguing.

"I keep another bag full of toys put away in the closet. Every now and then I switch these two bags. Then all of the old toys are new to him again. By the way, these are not expensive toys. A lot of nice empty small boxes and plastic bottles are included."

Here is a little fun for your **infant** "crawler" which will keep him occupied for hours.

Hang a shoe bag on the inside of his playpen. He will have a wonderful time putting his toys in the pockets and taking them out, putting them back in again, and so forth.

From New York: "I am sure you have all heard the old trick of putting a loud ticking clock in bed with a fussy puppy. Well, I tried it with my fussy **infant** and it really helped. The *only* trouble was that I forgot to turn off the alarm! My own absent-mindedness. I must admit things were a little hectic when it went off."

FOR THOSE UNINVITED GUESTS

From a man from Texas: "We have a redwood picnic table in our patio which we eat on almost nightly. As the patio is concrete, we have found that **insects** sometimes like to eat with us!

"My wife hit upon the idea of tying a piece of cloth around the bottom of each table leg and saturating it with insect repellent. This has been our answer to the ants. Have you got a better one?"

I think your wife's got a great idea. I have heard of people filling tin cans with water and setting each table leg in the cans of water before a picnic. I have actually seen this done and it does work. However, I am of the opinion that it might eventually rot the table legs.

Try taking tuna fish cans, washing them out, drying them thoroughly, and setting them under each of your table legs. Then fill them full of any kind of oil. An ant cannot possibly skim or crawl upon oil. We did this once in our yard. Our table stood over grass and this method worked like a charm. We also found that during mosquito season we could pour oil of citronella (bought at your drug store) in each can and the mosquitoes wouldn't come near us. Use only a teaspoon or so of oil of citronella in each can. How about that?

DON'T JOIN 'EM—BEAT 'EM!

Letter of laughter: "Here is my sneaky technique for exterminating the loathsome and wary bedroom fly or mosquito.

"Calmly turn off the light.

"Get the fly swatter.

"Go into the bathroom.

"Turn on the light.

"Wait patiently for a few minutes with fly swatter in hand.

"The **insect** will fly into the lighted room.

"Close the door and give the pest time to land.

"Swat it dead.

"Go back to bed and resume reading or sleeping in peace."

IRON WILL

Are you in the habit of **ironing** in your kitchen?

If so, why?

Take that ironing board to your living room and set it up in the prettiest spot in your house! After all, the living room contains most of your loveliest things, so why not enjoy them?

Just because Grandma called the living room her "parlor" —which was only for company and Sundays—does not mean that you shouldn't enjoy it yourself.

You will find that your ironing will become a pleasure when associated with your finest things—as your nice sofa, lamps and chairs. Besides, you will consider *yourself* "company" (which you certainly are) and find your ironing enjoyable instead of drudgery.

PADDED IRON SAVES HANDS

Many of you new brides write that your hands blister when you're doing the **ironing.** That's because they are not as old as mine! As the years pass, the blisters will turn into calluses. Later, the calluses will turn into toughened skin!

In the meantime (and by golly, that is now), I suggest that you take an old nylon stocking and wrap it around the handle of your electric iron. This will pad the handle.

Some people are allergic to nylon. If you wear nylon stockings and have not broken out, it is probably quite safe. If you can't stand the nylon, try wrapping the handle in a piece of soft wool. Some people like this even better as it is quite absorbent.

Cut the top and bottom off an old nylon stocking and, starting at one end of the handle, wrap the stocking around and around and around until you have a beautifully padded "handle." Then pin it with a safety pin or tack it with needle and thread.

And that's all there is to it! Not only does this padding cushion your ironing hand, but instead of moving your wrist every time, the nylon stocking will slip just enough to do *that* for you!

REVERSE YOURSELF FOR COMFORT

If you move the **ironed** portion of the item you are ironing away from you instead of toward you, I think you will find that you do not become nearly as warm as you do when pulling the hot ironed material toward you, which is the way I imagine most women iron. It will take practice to reverse the direction, but you'll be cooler.

WAXING ELOQUENT

For smoother ironing: "Never throw those small pieces of candles away. Put them on an old washrag and fold the rag over to form a packet.

"Put this on the end of your **ironing** board and swipe your iron against it as you iron those mountains of clothes each week. The iron will slide faster and easier. Save those muscles whenever you can, girls!"

FOR PRESSING PLASTIC

When you're **ironing** plastic material of any kind—such as curtains, etc.—if you use a piece of muslin from an old sheet on top of the plastic, the warm iron slides easily and does not stick to the plastic. The plastic keeps its softness this way, too.

GIVE THEM THE FLOOR

From Georgia: "A bedspread can be **ironed** in two or three minutes! Place the spread on a sheet-covered carpet in the middle of the floor and iron it on that. If you have a bare floor, it can be padded by spreading a blanket or quilt down first. This is also good for pressing curtains and draperies. It certainly beats using the ironing board and saves sags and puckers in the curtains and requires far less time and work."

TRY BROAD END OF BOARD

From Honolulu: "Here is a trick I discovered the other day when I had seven pairs of cafe curtains to **iron:**

"I turned my ironing board around and used the broad end instead of the tapered end. I was finished in half the time because I had a much larger surface and did not have to move the curtains as often.

"Many flat pieces, such as pillowcases, tablecloths, etc., can be done easier on this end of the board, too."

SHINE-PROOF PRESSING

From Houston: "Here's a way to **iron** men's woolen trousers, or any wool for that matter, without causing a shine.

"For a sharp crease, place ordinary newspaper on the ironing board and put the pants leg of the trouser on top of the newspaper. Carefully place the crease in its proper place. Then fold the newspaper around the crease and over the top of the trouser.

"Press with a fairly hot steam iron. The crease will be nice and sharp and there won't be a shine. The remaining parts of the trousers can also easily be pressed with the newspaper. Just tear the paper to smaller sizes for convenience. Saves pressing bills!

"Naturally, you press only *dark* trousers this way. For light-colored pants use a brown paper bag."

It is almost impossible to **iron** men's ties without shiny marks showing from the seams underneath.

To avoid this, cut a heavy flat-surfaced cardboard the proper shape and size of the tie and insert it under the outside smooth layer.

Results? No marks show on the tie!

TABLECLOTH TRICKS

From Kansas: "When I **iron** a tablecloth, I find that if I iron the middle of the cloth first, then fold it in half lengthwise and iron both sides, it not only lays straighter but also does not pucker when put on the table.

"Also, the center of the cloth is ironed while it is completely damp, and really, the center is what we notice most. If the edges of the cloth happen to be slightly dry, a few small wrinkles will not be so noticeable because the edges will hang over the side of the table.

"I never fold the cloth in half and crease that center fold with my iron. This not only wears out the cloth but makes it stick up in the middle—most unsightly.

"I was told that a cloth should be ironed out straight, folded once lengthwise down the middle and slightly—not heavily—ironed and that the folds, other than the center crease, should never be ironed. Can you brief me on this?"

I have looked in five etiquette books and as far as I can find out all five say this is the correct way to iron a cloth. One did say it was not necessary to crease the fold down the middle even with an iron—better to take your hand or finger and crease this fold! Immediately after the cloth is pressed it should be folded lengthwise first down the center. Then, the cloth should be folded over lengthwise again. The cloth may either be put on a coat hanger as is, or folded crosswise and laid in your linen chest.

USE CARD TABLE TO CATCH LINENS

From Long Island: "When **ironing** huge pieces of linen, such as tablecloths, sheets, etc., I get out my card table and place it flat on the floor under the ironing board. Do *not* unfold the legs. This way all of the clean linen hits the card table instead of the floor. If you really want to, and the ironing board is high enough, put the card-table legs up and set it under the board. However, I find that if it is placed flat on the floor, the cloth I am ironing *dries before* hitting the card table, thus avoiding more wrinkles.

"Another hot hint I found for ironing huge tablecloths was to open two legs of the card table and leave the other two folded up (put paper on the floor). This makes a slide for long tablecloths and sheets to go down and they automatically fold themselves by the time they hit the floor."

SPRINKLE OUT WRINKLES

From Texas: "I learned the most fantastic thing from my maid that should really be passed on to all **ironers:** her easy sprinkling method!

"Why do people sprinkle their clothes and then roll them up in a small ball? My mother and grandmother used to do this and so did I until a maid taught us to stack them loosely to save time and energy, and cut down on wrinkles.

"Use your kitchen table or drainboard. Lay the first garment *open* on the table. Take a clean vegetable brush and dip it in a bowl of *very* hot water and shake it above the article.

"Immediately put another garment on top of this one. The water on top of the first garment will be absorbed into the bottom of the second garment! Repeat process. Do *not* roll any clothes.

"Do the complete sprinkling job. Still do not fold or roll clothes. When all the sprinkling is done, lay two heavy bath towels on top of the clothes. If it will be a long time before you get around to ironing, sprinkle towels slightly.

"When ready to iron, no unrolling clothes and pressing wrinkles. Materials will be flat and time will be saved!"

GETTING THE STEAM UP

Don't sprinkle small items of clothing! Here is a time-saving idea:

Sprinkle a terry cloth bath towel with warm water, roll it up and let it absorb the moisture for a few minutes, then wrap the towel around the smaller end of your **ironing** board and pin it underneath.

This acts as a steam press and eliminates the problem of sprinkling and waiting for your clothes to get that perfect damp-dryness.

From Miami: "For those who have steam **irons** and are always having to guess the correct amount of water to put in them, I have found a way to eliminate all of the guessing and measuring.

"If you have an empty detergent bottle with the snip cap top, that is your answer.

"Take your empty bottle and some dark finger nail polish and make a line on both sides of the bottle which will indicate the proper amount of water to use each time."

HEAVEN SCENT

From Denver: "I always add a few drops of our favorite cologne before I pour the water into my steam **iron.**

"I have been doing this for years. So far it has never hurt the steam iron. All our clothes carry a pleasant fragrant odor, which seems to come from nowhere! Even our closets and chests of drawers smell lovely."

LONGER LIFE FOR IRONING BOARD COVERS

From Idaho: "I **iron** a knee patch (such as the kind ordinarily used on blue jeans) on the ironing board cover where my iron rests. This makes the cover last twice as long. When I see the patch beginning to wear, I take it off and iron on another patch. The iron goes over these patches smoothly even when I need to use *that* end of the ironing board!

"The patches can be bought in any dime store. This trick has saved replacing the cover so often."

From New York: "To make **ironing** a little easier, I slightly starch my ironing board cover. This also helps keep the cover clean longer."

From California: "After I wash and dry my muslin or twill **ironing board cover,** I put it back on the ironing board *wrong side up.* Reversing it after each laundering prolongs the wear because the side on the edge of the board from which a person irons becomes *more* scorched and wears faster."

From Delaware: "When your bottom contour sheets wear out, use them for **ironing board covers.** Just rip them in two. The contour corner fits the neck of the ironing board and is made to order! Cut to size and tack or use ironing board pins on the rest of it. It works beautifully."

MANY A JEWEL OF AN IDEA HERE

From Montreal: "For those who have silver **jewelry** which darkens upon exposure to air: I have found that I can put my bracelets, necklace and earrings in a waxed paper sandwich bag, roll the bag up and place it in my drawer.

"Not only does the waxed paper bag keep the silver from tarnishing, but I can see the pair of earrings, bracelet, etc., I am looking for."

From Maine: "When my imitation pearl beads and earrings turn yellow from wear, I dye them any color I choose.

"I just mix dye in a little jar, drop in the **jewelry** and let it stand—shaking it once in a while—until the desired color has been absorbed. Sure is pretty."

From Pennsylvania: "Here is a **jewelry** goodie I will pass on to you. Go to the hardware store and buy the finest fishing line and use it to restring your broken necklaces. Works like a charm. You can string the pearls you hadn't had any luck with when a needle wouldn't go through. The nylon is firm enough so that you don't need a needle, but soft enough to hang beautifully."

From Hollywood: "Our daughter has many necklaces and bracelets. If kept in a large **jewelry** box, they become quite tangled. We spent much time and effort getting the knots out of the chains and trying to keep them separated, until I went to a variety store and (since her room is all pink) purchased a pink plastic 'stick-on' curtain rod. Now she hangs each necklace and bracelet over the rod and closes the clasp! Each article is then ready to remove and, best of all, no matted chains.

"I put the rod on her closet door. The total cost was twenty-nine cents.

"For ladies with many assorted earrings, a ten-cent round curtain rod works wonderfully. Try it, and your jewelry problems will be solved."

Plastic ice cube trays in a **jewelry** drawer are wonderful for keeping earrings easily accessible and neat. Each pair can have its own little compartment.

LET THAT KITCHEN CLUTTER GO, GO, GO!

Let's discuss the **kitchen drawer,** where we all keep our daily clutter accumulated.

This is the drawer, ordinarily next to the kitchen stove, where we keep our favorite knives and spoons and no telling what else.

While you are reading this, think to yourself, "Now, what *is* in that drawer?" (Bet you can't make a complete list before you look!)

How much of it is really necessary? What do you actually need? Can you find your favorite knife immediately? And spoon?

When you clean the drawer, do you just remove all the "stuff," get the crumbs out, line it with new paper and replace everything and let it go?

Don't!

You will be right back where you started—still having to knock everything aside to find that favorite spoon or knife.

Put some newspaper down on the drainboard and literally pour out everything in the drawer into the paper.

Just look at all that excess junk and clutter! Whatever do you need *all* this mess for? You have only two hands. There are umpteen spoons and only four burners on the stove. How could anyone use umpteen spoons at one time?

Wipe out the drawer and line it, whether it be with newspaper, a paper sack or bag, adhesive-backed paper, cardboard, foil, wax paper, etc.

Now . . . don't throw all that stuff *back* in the drawer. Stop, look and *think,* What do I really use every day?

Pick out your favorite butcher knife, paring knife, spatula,

97

egg turner, can opener and not more than four spoons. Replace these in your drawer.

Where you will probably have your downfall is when it comes to the spoons. Just how many spoons do you have in that cluttered drawer? Six or eight, perhaps.

Now, you are going to say, "But I have had these spoons for years and can't throw them away." You don't have to. If they have sentimental value, get a paper bag and put all these excess items in it. Test yourself.

Put the bag with all these excess items in the garage or closet. If you don't go into that old kitchen grab-bag within a week, then it's a fact that you can do without those extra gadgets. If you decide later you must have a certain item, it's always there.

How many bottle openers do you have? About six? You can open only one bottle or can at a time. We keep them because we think someday one might not work. We can still open only one bottle or can at a time so pick out the best two and put them back in the drawer.

Go through all your equipment this way.

What you can do without, you don't need. Get rid of it so you can find something quickly. Saves your time and nerves. Eliminates excess cleaning, clutter, etc.

Don't faint when you see how little will be in this favorite drawer after this cleaning. It pays off.

You will have a glorious feeling tomorrow when you open the drawer and find what you are looking for immediately.

Simplicity is the answer to our problems.

GET OUT HIDDEN DIRT

From Georgia: "Just how does one keep the little space on top of the **kitchen cabinets** clean? It's so high that I seldom see it. Recently I got on a cleaning jag and what a mess I found."

Never leave this shelf uncovered, whether your cabinets are wooden or metal.

Waxed paper is cheap! Once the shelf is clean, tear off a long sheet or two of the wax paper and, after "sprinkling" your cabinet with a bit of water so the paper will hold down and not slip, cover the shelf quickly.

I then add a second sheet of wax paper and the next time

I am in that fanatical mood all I have to do is remove the top paper, and my shelves are clean again. You can also use the synthetic bags which come from the dry cleaners. They are *free* and adhere beautifully.

SIMPLE AS A, B, C

From a happy cook: "On my spice rack, to make the spices easier to find, I arrange them alphabetically. This is a real **kitchen** time-saver!"

TEND TO YOUR KNITTING!

For those who **knit** or crochet: I have found that you can take a wide-mouthed mayonnaise jar and put the ball of yarn or thread into the jar. Take your ice pick and punch a big hole in the top of the lid.

After putting the yarn inside the jar, thread it through this hole.

You will find that this will keep the yarn clean, it won't tangle and get mixed up with other things, and the weight of the jar keeps it from rolling all over the floor.

To wind a hank of **knitting** yarn or crochet thread, place the hank over a lamp shade, unscrew the top ornament until it is free from the shade, and the shade turns as you wind your yarn. No tangles!

A note to **knitters:** If you take a cork from any bottle top and place it on the pointed ends of your knitting needles when you lay your knitting aside, there will be no dropped stitches to worry about.

If you take a soap-filled scouring pad and rub your wooden **knitting** needle with it, your knitting thread will work like magic! You can knit twice as fast this way.

TAKING THE UGH! OUT OF LAUNDRY DAY

Laundry! That is the bane of every housewife's existence. I know what housewives go through. I have a six-room house and children to take care of, too.

There are many ways to do laundry. Daily, weekly, and just not at all! I have never figured out the answer to that last point!

If any of you have a real answer to this problem, let me know and I will send you an orchid. Until then, the best way that I know of is to buy less and less clothing that needs to be ironed. This cuts down on the most depressing part of housework. You and I know that while the washing is bad enough, the ironing is what makes us tired and, *ugh!*

LET THE DRIP-DRIES SAVE YOU WORK

Did you know that tablecloths can be bought now in pure dacron? These never need ironing. You can find also drip-dry nylon, dacron and all "ons" in underwear, slips, blankets, jackets, dresses and just about everything.

Buy them! They're worth every extra dime that you pay. Why? Because you will not spend your time at the ironing board doing dreary work that is not only time-consuming but also labor- and energy-using! Ladies, save your energy, soap, time and nerves any way you can! This will keep you young and soon you will begin to look objectively at things!

All these man-made fabrics need to be treated correctly or they will be a disappointment. Learn to wash them in your machine. But remember: they have their own secrets.

A man-made fabric does not have the attributes of cotton, wool, etc. Nor does it react like them. Synthetics have no pores. They are not spun together. They are made with chemicals and many other things; therefore, they cannot be handled like linen and cotton.

If you buy something labeled synthetic, read the label carefully. It will give you the directions. I prefer the word "secrets," for they are the almost miraculous answer to all the letters I get which complain, "It said washable and no-iron, but it's awful. Even after ironing I could not remove the wrinkles." That's because it was washed in too hot water! Watch it.

If you wash in a top-loading washing machine, turn the water on hot, dump in your soap, and as soon as about three inches of water are in the machine, turn the hot water *off* and finish filling with cold water.

If you have a side-loader, forget the above. Use lukewarm water and *never* spin dry! This sets the wrinkles. Man-made fabrics do not have to have the dirt washed *out* of them. Would you use scalding water to wash a window which has no pores?

WASH THOSE GOOD DRESSES BY HAND

Once in a while we housewives will splurge and buy an expensive drip-dry dress. After it has become soiled, our problem is: Shall we take the chance and wash it? Or shall we splurge again and send it to the cleaners to keep it looking nice?

In the past I have ruined many drip-dry dresses by washing them incorrectly.

I feel that today I can give you an honest answer to the question of how to wash these good dresses correctly. I have one dress that has been washed seventeen times. It was guaranteed to be drip-dry. Today it still looks perfect and has never been ironed.

The best place to wash this type of dress is in the bathtub. Fill the tub with about two inches of *lukewarm* water. Add some liquid detergent and mix it throughout the water. (If your dress is stained—maybe with perspiration—soak the dress in absolutely cold tap water first.)

Lay the dress out full length in the bathtub. Let it remain no longer than eight minutes in the detergent water.

Take your vegetable brush or any hairbrush, and holding

the shoulder of the dress in your left hand, brush the dress from top to bottom. Pay special attention to the neckline marks on the collar and lapels. These areas can be given a special scrubbing. Be *sure* to hold your dress *under* water when brushing these areas. By holding the dress completely under water as you brush, the particles of soil become loosened and the soil gets into the water.

Pull the drain plug from the bathtub. Turn on both water faucets again to get lukewarm water, making your mixture with the two faucets. Hold up the dress by its neckline *under* the water faucet for a moment so you will get a strong flush of water directly on the neckline. That will rinse the fibers of the material thoroughly. Rinsing is a necessity when it comes to getting soap film and suds from clothing.

Hold the dress up after rinsing most of the suds off so that it will drain. While gathering the dress at the waistline in one hand, after the water has drained out of the tub, put the plug back in the tub and turn on the water faucets again to get more lukewarm water.

Dip the dress into the bathtub, and using your brush scrub the dress thoroughly from the top to the bottom.

This may take two rinsings—depending on how soiled your dress is—and if two rinsings are used, I have *never* found any type of material that could possibly be hurt by adding a half-cup of vinegar to the last rinse water. This removes soap film. It also removes perspiration odors.

While your dress is *under* the last rinse water, approximately two inches deep, place a plastic coat hanger in the neck of the dress. Then and only then, lift it up from the water by the neck of the coat hanger. The weight of the water will pull all wear wrinkles out of the dress itself.

While it is still dripping wet, hang it on the shower nozzle. This will allow the water to drip into the tub.

After the dress is hung, take your fingers and gently move the skirt, in case it has stuck together. Most materials do stick, so carefully place the gathered or pleated skirt into its correct position.

After seventeen washings, the dress that I mentioned to you has never needed to be ironed.

I have gone into lots of detail to tell you how to do this. But the entire procedure takes only about three minutes. So don't think it is a difficult operation. Husbands' shirts and kiddies' drip-dries may be laundered the same way.

Remember these things when washing expensive drip-dry articles:

Never use hot water.

Never soak too long.

Never use too much soap.

Never wring the dress.

Rinse well, and hang correctly.

GETTING THE HANG OF IT

After trying many methods for hanging **laundry,** I think I've come up with the best. I was wasting time (and seconds count if there's a pile of them) by separating the load of laundry as I placed it on the clothesline.

I took a stop watch and timed nineteen batches of laundry. Each hanging included five loads, which the average lines hold. I found that it is far better to pick up whatever has come from the washing machine and is in the laundry basket unsorted, give it a big snap, and then hang it above the point nearest the laundry basket.

Why? Because the washing machine has mixed up all the clothing and it takes too long to dig into the basket to find a pillowslip that belongs with another pillowslip and hang them next to each other.

It is far better to hang your five loads of laundry any old way and then, after it is dry, take it down the way you want to sort it. In the first place, your clothes are not wet then and they are not nearly so heavy. This saves lots of energy. If you doubt this, weigh a basket of wet laundry before you hang it up and then weigh it when it's dry!

Now, when you take the laundry off the line, first remove the articles which require tedious ironing and starching. Put these in the *bottom* of your basket.

Next, go along the line and pick off the things which require very little ironing, such as your pillowslips, etc. On top of this basketload, lay your husband's underwear. Then your dish towels and bath towels—the bath towels will give your laundry basket a new flat surface and a better level to put the other things on and prevent further wrinkles.

Next take down all of your socks, etc. When you remove socks you will save time if, as you pick one sock off the line, you find its mate and fold them together, thus saving mating them later. Now, put your drip-dries on top of all this.

Of course this procedure is not to be construed as something one *has* to do. Do it any way you like, because I do not know what you iron and what you don't iron. The one great thing about this method is the psychological effect it has on the housewife:

When you go into the house you can either have your family help put the top clothes away or you can put them away yourself. Under any circumstance, once the top clothes are put away your basket looks almost empty.

You'll be so happy that your basket is half unloaded that you'll want to get at the ironing in a hurry!

CUT LAUNDRY COSTS

From California: "I tried to wash and iron a lovely tablecloth, but the cloth puckered. It took hours, too! The laundry is so expensive. Please tell me how to **launder** these cloths . . . or I will eat off a bare table."

Talk with your laundry man to see if he can help you.

Put the cloth in *with* your regular laundry and have it "done" by the pound . . . flat-work finished. Laundries charge so much for flat work according to what it *weighs*.

When your cloth comes home, you will find that it is *not* nicely done and looks as if it had been run through a mangle. It won't be perfect, but don't despair! You had it done cheaply.

Get out your ironing board (better yet, I use the floor in the living room and spread down a quilt), take an ice cube and run it over the wrinkles and the edge of the cloth. Let this soak in for a few minutes and then use your iron and just press the wrinkles out! You'll save money, time, energy and puckering.

This is called spot-ironing or "hand-finishing," which you are charged a fortune for if someone else does it! Do you know that many nurses have their uniforms done "regular," and then hand-finish them this way?

I had a good laundry man tell me all this when I complained about the charge for my cloths. Another thing he taught me was that I could wash many things myself and send them to him for steam pressing. Cuts expense that way, too.

Be sure that you include bath towels, etc., with the cloth so it will be classed as "flat work" and you won't be charged for "piece work."

CURTAINS FOR THE BIRDS

While testing **laundry** methods at a friend's house, I hit upon a good idea:

There happened to be quite a few birds in the neighborhood, so, as soon as I hung up the clothes, I took an old plastic shower curtain and spread it across the top of the four clotheslines umbrella fashion . . . and clipped the four corners tightly with clothespins. The plastic curtain protects the laundry from the birds and may be hosed off later. (This is especially good for women who leave their clothes out airing for more than one day. I've found that if I left my white things out two days they were even whiter. The moisture, which comes around midnight, seeps into the white sheets, pillowcases, bath towels, and diapers, and just does something to the clothes.

NO SLIP WHILE THEY DRIP

From Arizona: "My husband went to an old secondhand place and bought a length of chain. He wired this between my two clothesline poles.

"When I hang out my **laundry** I now put all my drip-dries on coat hangers and place the neck of each hanger in a link of the chain.

"By doing this, I do not have to worry about my clothes

falling off the line or sliding down to one end of the wire and getting matted."

From Texas: "I use shower curtain hooks to attach my pants-stretchers (for cotton trousers) to the **laundry** line. This was my husband's idea. It's really great."

MAYBE YOUR MACHINE'S JUST THIRSTY

Three of my neighbors couldn't get their **laundry** white. I noticed there wasn't as much water in their washing machines as in mine. *That* was the trouble. Naturally when we wash ten pounds of clothes, there is supposed to be a definite amount of water. *Test* your own machine.

Look at the manual that came with the washer (or call the salesman who sold it to you and ask him), and you will see that you are supposed to have so many gallons of water in each machine-load of laundry.

Here's how we tested these machines. We measured the water as it came out of the drain hose! One machine was supposed to hold nine gallons and it gave us only seven! In one machine, we found the water shortage was caused by low pressure. The other two machines needed adjusting. If your machine is the type in which you can measure the water, do so.

Remember, you can't wash your hair in one teacup of water, either! So the fault may lie in a water shortage if you're not getting clean clothes.

CUT DOWN ON YOUR SOAKING

From a friend in Washington: "Why do you say to soak clothes only ten minutes? I always soak mine overnight in suds and bleach."

Home economists tell me that after clothes soak fourteen minutes the dirt is loose. After that time, the dirt in the water starts soaking back into the clothes. I take their word for it . . . **laundry** is their business. Besides, I've tested it!

When I tell you to soak your clothes only ten minutes, I know what I'm doing. When your bell goes off to tell you the ten minutes are up, you may be in the bath, wiping a child's face, or on the phone. Then it takes another three or four minutes to dry off or find your cigarettes or say goodbye and get back to the laundry.

Ten minutes is sufficient time for soaking clothes. If you leave them sixteen minutes, the dirt will begin setting back into them! The water is soiled by that time. Just think, what would it be like if you took a perfectly clean white shirt and soaked it in dirty water? It would get gray!

Don't soak clothes in dirty water. This is why people who have old-type manual machines always wash their white clothes first, coloreds next, and then dark things. Remember how dirty the water in the washtubs used to be by the time you washed the colored things? Same thing with soaking! And don't forget the soap film. If your clothes are white before ironing and then turn gray, it's soap film. Remove it.

RUST-PROOF YOUR WASHING

From Hawaii: "I am a military man, living on an island where we have rust in our water. And what a **laundry** problem that is! I was told nothing could be done about it, so I did a little detective work and found something that might be of help to housewives whose clothes turn yellow from rust in the water.

"I went to the local laundry because they were the only ones who could get our laundry really clean and white.

"I found them using thick cotton pads over the hydrant where the water poured into the machine. The pads would immediately turn yellow-looking and have to be replaced often. The pads gathered the iron in the laundry water and the owner told me that he must remove the iron this way to prevent the clothes from becoming yellow.

"I then went back to my quarters and folded an old terry cloth bath towel over the end of the hose and held it tight as the water ran into our washing machine. The towel turned the color of a walnut table! The terry cloth strains the water and catches the iron rust.

"We also learned *not* to use soap. We found that a detergent was far better! I don't know what it does, but it works."

I have had people write to me saying that when their water pipes were rusty or they had an old water heater which gave out rust, they put a big terry cloth bath towel in the washing machine and let it swish around for a few minutes, then removed the towel before dumping in their **laundry.** That works, too!

WHITE ON WHITE

From Connecticut: "I keep my white nylon slips and blouses, resin-finished cottons, and dacrons white by **laundering** them all together—whether sheets or shirts—regardless of material. I use hot water and perborate bleach, *never* a chlorine bleach with my detergents."

TRY THIS

From a mother: "If you have no clothesline or the line is already full of the weekly **laundry,** use baby's playpen to dry diapers, either inside or outside the house."

SPRAY TREATMENT FOR JEANS

From San Francisco: "Before **laundering** stained and muddy blue jeans, I put them out on the grass and spray them for a few minutes with my garden hose, nozzle turned to 'strong.' This leaves the dirt on the *ground* instead of *in* the washing machine!"

ROLL AWAY CREASES

From New York: "Save the cardboard tubes from paper towels, waxed paper, etc. Tape as many of these together as necessary, maybe the width of your blankets or drapes. Take a knife and slit the cardboard tubes on one side only and slip over your **laundry** line.

"I find this is wonderful for keeping creases out of towels, blankets, T-shirts, sweaters and the like where they hang over the line. You can pull the article either way after hanging it on the line, as the tubes roll."

SALT BOXES KEEP LAUNDRY ROOM TIDY

From New Hampshire: "The other day I decided to clean up my **laundry room**. I had just looked at the shelves, full of half-empty boxes, wet boxes, soiled boxes and different-colored boxes!

"I had saved a bunch of empty salt boxes, the ones with the little pouring spout on the side. I covered these with contact paper (foil could be used). The foil or plastic type of paper will keep the box from getting dirty or soiled. It also keeps the box itself from absorbing water.

"I then took my old bottle of fingernail polish and labeled the side of each box: bleach, detergent, etc. I now find my laundry room is such a pleasure to work in and so clean that I actually flit down the stairs to do my laundry.

"One good thing about salt boxes is that the tops can be removed easily for replacements. Most things (except laundry powder) will fit into a one-pound salt box. I keep the big box of soap or detergent underneath my shelf so it won't look cluttery."

SECRETS OF THE NOT-SO-INSCRUTABLE ORIENT

From California: "I am an Oriental antique dealer. Nearly everything in my shop is **lacquer** finished. I am willing to share the Chinese secret of cleaning and preserving **lacquer.**

"Take three-fourths of a cup of water, put it in a pan and bring it to a rolling boil. Put two tea bags in this. Put a tight lid on the pan and let the tea steep. Shake the pan around until the tea bag is well soaked. Leave the lid *on* the pan until the tea is cold.

"Now . . . be sure to remove *all* of the waxes and oils from the lacquered pieces. Dry *thoroughly*. Take a terry cloth rag and dip into the cold tea. Apply this briskly to all the lacquered pieces.

"Now, here's the secret—do *not* wipe this off! The tea contains tannic acid. The tannic acid will return the lacquer to its original gloss!

"Lacquer needs no waxes, oils, etc. In fact, it is the Oriental opinion of one who deals in these lovely finishes—whether new or old—that oils and waxes should never be applied to them."

NEW LIFE FOR OLD LAMP SHADES

Recently, for the first time in my life, I washed silk **lamp shades.** I completely ruined one . . . and now let me tell you how to prevent this from happening to you!

Don't wash the shade if it is years old or if the fabric has rotted! Four years ago, I bought four beautiful matching shades. Only one is ruined. That was the shade that had been by the open window where the sun was shining on it most of the time. I believe the sun coming through the glass rotted the fabric.

If possible, rotate your lamp shades at least once a year. Especially with pairs, because matching shades are quite expensive. If the shades on a pair of matching lamps are rotated . . . at least they will wear out at the same time. We don't feel so bad about this, but to have an odd one makes us sick!

Now, from all the letters sent in on how to wash lamp shades (and some were hilarious), I compiled four different methods. Here's the best:

First, look to see if your fabric is sewn on the frame. Most are.

Never wash a lamp shade or even try to spot clean it before removing the dust. Either use a vacuum cleaner and draw the dust out—and I find this best—or take a *clean* brush and brush the shade well. Then, and only then, get ready to wash it.

If your sink is big enough, fill it with lukewarm water. If not, use your tub. Add a mild detergent to the water. Mix this well.

My shades were white silk taffeta and had a gimp trim. Trims are sometimes loose. Take a needle and thread and tack any loose places with a loose basting or blind-stitch. When gimp is glued on, warm water will sometimes cause it to come loose. On my shades, it came loose in only one place, and I later glued it back on.

If the trim on your shade is a different color from the shade itself, I suggest you remove the trim (it's easy). Otherwise, it might fade.

And, ladies, if your gimp (or trim) is bad, forget it. New gimp can be bought at upholstery shops and it is very cheap. Besides, this may be just what you are looking for to give those shades new zip. It's easy to glue or tack on with a needle and thread.

Drape an old nylon stocking (you'll use this later) around your neck and lay a bath towel on the drainboard. Put the lamp shade in the suds and immediately wet the entire shade to prevent spotting and rings. This can be done by twirling the shade through the water or taking a glass and pouring the water over the shade.

Use a soft, clean vegetable brush and *gently* rub the fabric. This should be done as quickly as possible. You do not want the shade in the water too long. You want to prevent rust and not dissolve some types of glue.

Rinse well with a spray. Hair sprays attached to the kitchen faucet are grand for this. If you have no spray, take the shade to your bathroom and rinse it in the tub. By holding your finger under the spigot you can have a pretty good spray substitute. Or take a glass of water and pour the water through the shade.

Immediately after rinsing, put the shade on the bath towel. This will absorb some of the water that has come to the bottom of the shade. Rinsing is most important. You do not want any soap film left in the shade. One woman used vinegar water for rinsing . . . that works well.

Now take the shade outside to the clothesline. Grab that nylon stocking you've had hanging around your neck and tie it to the brace on top of the shade, then tie the stocking to the clothesline.

You may look like you belong in an institution when you hang lampshades on a clothesline (my neighbors laughed), but the wind and air will dry them quickly and prevent rust. Do this on only a hot, dry day.

When the shades are dry—and it won't take very long—glue or sew on any gimp or trim that might have come loose.

For those who live in apartments and don't have clotheslines, I have another idea, which I used on one shade:

After most of the water is absorbed by the towel, put the shade back on the lamp, turn on the light and set up an electric fan so that it will blow on the shade. The heat from the light and the air from the fan will dry it. I suggest putting the lamp and shade on the floor on a newspaper so if a drip of water falls it will not spot your table. (Preventive measures!)

And, ladies, if you are tired of white (or tired of yellowed lampshades), tint 'em! Mix a big tub of water colored with a good all-purpose dye and swish the shades in it. Real pretty.

I know one thing: From now on, I will wash my lampshades when they are soiled and not let fly specks accumulate or the fabric rot. Dust *does* cause rotting.

And by the way, as the shades dry, they will shrink and become tight on the frame again, so don't worry if your shades pucker a bit at first.

I would like to issue one word of caution to you if you have bought a new lamp shade. Remove the cellophane strips on it (which usually are wrapped around the shade to prevent dust marks).

You are probably keeping the cellophane on your lamp shade to protect it from dust. Don't do it. When the sun shines in your home it will make dark streaks on your lamp shade. To prevent streaks, dark places and warp, always remove the cellophane wrapping as soon as you bring the shade home.

This advice comes from manufacturers of lamp shades. How can we doubt their word? Let's not even try. They are educated in this field. We aren't. Why let a pretty lamp shade warp?

From Maine: "For those who have old paper-covered and fabric-covered **lamp shades** (with paper lining), may I tell you how I renovate all of our shades? I am in this business.

"Dust the shade *well* inside and out with a brush.

"Paint the inside of the shade with any paint that happens to be about the house. (Use a brush.) You should use a black, dark gray, dark brown or aluminum paint. I prefer aluminum, but often use black. Let this dry overnight.

"Now paint *over* the dark color on the *inside* of the shade with white or any pastel paint. I always use a *non-shiny, flat* paint. Amazingly enough, one coat invariably covers perfectly. Hang the shade with a string on a clothesline to thoroughly dry.

"Now for the last operation:

"Paint the outside of the open shade any color you wish. One coat of flat paint only. Then let hang to dry once again.

"Result? New shades that can be sponged off when soiled.

"If a contrasting trimming is desired, buy some at a dime store; quarter-inch velvet ribbon is very attractive. Stationery stores sell 'paper' narrow banding in colors and metallics, so often found on new shades. If you are planning to use new trim, the old trim should be pulled off before painting. The new bindings may be applied with glue.

"Reason for the dark colors on the inside: If a dark color is not applied first you will have an unpleasant shade when lighted. Every brush stroke will show up.

"After using this method you will no longer have a translucent shade, but an opaque one. Many of the finest lamps are fitted with new opaque shades and give excellent lighting."

From Duluth: "I found directions in a farm magazine for cleaning parchment **lamp shades.** It recommended using rubbing alcohol applied with a piece of absorbent cotton in a gentle circular motion. You should work slowly and patiently, covering small areas at a time."

BETTER LEATHER LONGER

From Connecticut: "I work in the office of a tannery and the phone rings frequently with people asking for advice about their **leather**-topped furniture. They usually say someone left or spilled an alcoholic drink on the leather table top and it bleached the leather white and 'What can I do?' Or, 'Is it possible to re-dye it exactly?'

"They might try this:

"Clean the entire top of the table with saddle soap and let it dry *completely.*

"*Sparingly,* apply a scuff-type liquid polish to the affected area, using a color that matches as closely as possible. If it should stain the leather too dark, pour the polish on a clean cloth and lightly coat the entire top of the table, to more or less even the color.

"Another frequent question: 'Can I use varnish or similar products on my leather table tops?'

"The answer to this is *No!* Leather is skin and as such must 'breathe.' It contains fats and oils introduced in tanning processes to keep it glowing and alive looking. These are all that are necessary to the finish.

"If your table top has lost its gloss, it most likely is dirty. Again, use saddle soap to clean it! It should be cleaned this way at least every six months. Saddle soap contains the essential oils which leather needs.

"And as a parting word of caution, if you must polish leather for any reason, use only leather dressing polishes sold by most better furniture stores."

CAUTION IS THE WORD IN LINEN STORAGE

When you store your little-used **linens** . . . and this means putting away baby dresses for the next generation, or that beautiful tablecloth you only use once a year or so . . . I recommend that you do *not* starch and iron them first.

The thing to do is to wash them and rinse *thoroughly*.

Place out in the sunlight to dry (if at all possible) and put them away unironed. This way, they will not have any starch in them, or *ironed* wrinkles.

Ironed wrinkles or folds, when left in linens that are stored a year or so, break down the fibers and then—because the fabrics have not been rinsed—accumulate vapors, odors and bad creases.

It is my suggestion that when you store these precious things, you rinse them not once, but two or three times.

I recommend putting a half-cup of vinegar in the last rinse water. This will eliminate soap film (and it is only my opinion, but I'll stick behind it), which causes deterioration and yellowing of stored materials.

So . . . wash the articles, rinse, rinse *again* in vinegar water, dry thoroughly, put out in the sunshine to dry and then wrap in tissue paper and store.

The material will be wrinkled. So? Who cares? Why waste energy ironing it today, folding it and tucking it away? You may not use it for years!

When precious things like linens and keepsakes are stored, they should be gone through at least once a year. Here's why:

Sometimes they begin to yellow. This is usually aging, and since you haven't starched and ironed the material, just throw it in the laundry again. You are preventing rotting, aging, and deterioration of the lovely article.

You and I both know that we don't use these things very often. I have had women send me gorgeous table linens (please *don't* send me yours! I can't possibly return these things) that some sweet grandmother had washed, starched and ironed and stowed away in a cedar chest. Wow, such messes! All caused from improper rinsing (soap film), starch, ironing and laying away too long without rewashing.

When you store these articles, I suggest that you buy any brand of bar soap on the market, *remove* the wrapper and place the bars of soap in the closet. This will help prevent that musty odor which often accumulates on stored linens. Besides, you can always use the soap in a pinch!

With all we have to do, aren't you glad you have an excuse *not* to iron that big cloth today?

m

LET'S MAKE UP!

Have you been wondering what to do with your old jars and tubes of foundation **make-up** now that one-step matte-finish make-up is available?

I take a jar, tube or bottle of any foundation cream, add to it a proportionate amount of my favorite face powder, mixing well until entirely absorbed. The cream will absorb more than you would imagine and still remain creamy.

This mixture can be applied to the face very neatly and works as well as any matte make-up I have ever tried. It is a tremendous money-saver for women.

Just recently I experimented with the following idea which I thought might be helpful to other women concerning their wardrobes:

Before removing dresses, blouses or sweaters over your head, place an old shower cap over your face (underneath your chin and above your forehead), and thus avoid any **make-up** rubbing into your garments.

HANDS ACROSS THE TABLE

Most of us do our own **manicures**. At least I do. But about once a year I go hog wild and go to a beauty shop and get "the works"! I did recently.

But I sure got my money's worth. I talked and asked questions till I captured some top secrets to share with you. Namely, why manicures last so long when professionally done.

Here are some basic rules that were given to me:

Nails are composed of horny layers of dead cells held together by the substance called keratin. Nails tend to split and

117

peel when this is destroyed by detergents or constant pounding such as typing. Sometimes illness or drugs taken internally can affect the nails.

Fingernails should be kept as uniformly in shape as possible. They should be kept oval or round for some jobs, such as typing, etc. Otherwise, they should be tapered but never should be filed to a sharp point.

Nails need not be conspicuously long to be beautiful. Uniformity of length and soft, pliable-looking cuticles are what give hands true appeal.

Don't neglect nails and cuticles for weeks at a time and suddenly go to work on them with a vengeance!

Forcing the cuticle back by using too much pressure can cause injury, such as inflammation at the base of the nail or dents and white spots. Long neglect and over-ambition could defeat the entire purpose.

Keep nails smooth at all times with an emery board.

Use glycerine, cuticle remover or lotion and massage around the cuticle, gently and gradually pushing it back. Avoid over-friction.

If cuticles are very tight and cling to the base of the nails, soak in warm vinegar water (half-and-half) for five minutes. Then apply glycerine and rub with a blunt orange stick.

If there are hangnails (broken skin), trim them with cuticle scissors and be sure to trim as close as possible.

Remember, the cuticle around the nail is holding the skin of the finger together! When the cuticle is cut away or broken, the skin around the nails rolls back and causes more hangnails! Never cut cuticles unless absolutely necessary.

Rinse nails with warm water, using a small brush, and then gently rub them dry.

Before applying nail polish, take a small piece of cotton, dip in vinegar (yep, plain old household vinegar) and wipe each fingernail. This will not only leave the nails absolutely clean but will also make them more pliable . . . and the polish will adhere to the nails longer.

If you can't apply colored fingernail polish neatly, it is far better to use clear polish and use a white pencil under the nails. Wet the pencil before using.

Correct procedure for applying polish is: one base coat (that's the white, clear stuff, gals), two coats of polish and one top coat. This is the accepted method today and if you follow it your polish will last longer.

And here's another hint that this professional manicurist threw in!

If women would apply a little glycerine (this can be bought at any drugstore) on the hands and massage it in well before applying hand cream or lotions, the results will be amazing.

To remove the "sticky" feeling after applying the glycerine, just run a little water over the hands and pat them lightly with a soft towel. This will leave the hands soft and smooth for hours.

And, gals, there's no reason that we can't have good looking nails. The dime stores are loaded with tools and stuff to do them with. Quite inexpensive, too. Brace up, and make yourself feel good with a professional manicure that costs you practically nothing!

SOLUTION FOR CLEANING MAHOGANY

From Toledo: "Here is a hint for those who have **mahogany** bedroom furniture:

"I have never used furniture polish on it. I make suds from baby soap and use the suds to wash the mahogany. To rinse it, I mix one-half cup of vinegar to one gallon of water, and use a damp cloth. Then I dry the furniture thoroughly.

"Some of my friends use one-third cup of vinegar to two quarts of water and polish the furniture with a cloth wrung out of this mixture."

From Nevada: "I have a beautiful cherry **mahogany** bedroom set and accidentally spilled some alcohol on it and did not realize it, and it set all day long.

"I thought pecan meat [ladies, this is the inside of the pecan] would only work on water marks, but almost as if by magic the stain was gone after rubbing it with the pecan.

"This saved me an expensive refinishing job."

CONTOURS FOR MATTRESS PADS

From South Dakota: "I modernized my **mattress** pads (I bought mine before contour pads came into being) by taking contour sheets that were worn too thin in the center for further use and pinning my mattress pads to them while they were on the bed.

"I removed the sheets and pads from the beds and brought them to my sewing machine with the pins still in . . . then I stitched each pad to the old contour sheet.

"Then I cut the old, worn parts from the center of the contour sheet to prevent puckers. This raw edge of the sheet may be turned under and stitched again for either strength or neatness.

"This left me with a pad in the center and the thin contour sheet to hold it down and keep it from sliding. It's excellent, easy to put on the bed and doesn't wrinkle.

"The 'contour' parts of the sheet were still strong enough for many more months' use."

TO MAKE A MERRY MEAT LOAF

I have tried all ways of cooking **meat loaf.**

I have made little, individual meat loaves (especially for the freezer) and have also put them in muffin tins for freezing or cooking. Now, I want to tell you of another method a wonderful friend wants to share with us.

She suggests cutting the tops out of fruit-juice cans and using them for baking our meat loaves. When the loaves are cold, they slice beautifully. Also, this method eliminates having to wash a greasy roaster!

You can use regular fruit-juice cans or those little frozen-juice cans.

The small frozen fruit-juice cans make tiny meat loaves which I cooked, let cool and later froze. These are great when company drops in or for canapés. Just cut the bottom of the can out with your opener and push the small frozen meat loaves out. Cut in thin slices. These can either be served cold or heated and laid on a platter as the main dish for a meal, or put on crackers for snacks, etc.

After these individual meat loaves have been cooked in the tins in your oven and cooled *thoroughly,* wrap them in foil and put them in your deep freeze.

If you are going to serve the meat loaves at a buffet party, try putting some chili powder in the mixture before baking.

This gives a tang all its own. Better yet, when you make the meat loaves, put chili powder in only *half* of the meat before cooking, and you will have two kinds of party foods!

Here's another tip if you want to be real fancy and different: After the tiny meat loaves thaw slightly, take a piece of waxed paper and sprinkle paprika on it. *Roll* the meat loaves in this *before* cutting. Then when you cut the slices . . . you will have a thin *red* edge around your miniature meat loaf! On one can I mixed a dab of chili powder in the paprika. Made it really hot!

Be sure to pack your little cans pretty full, because if the hamburger meat is very fat, it will shrink slightly. Happy eating!

Have you ever tried baking **a meat loaf** in your angel food cake pan? It's terrific!

I sometimes use this method when freezing meat loaves. The reason for it:

As long as I am making up a meat loaf recipe I always make enough for two. I set the second half of the meat loaf mixture in my refrigerator until the first meat loaf is cooked.

By cooking it in an angel food cake pan I find it cooks *much* faster. The hole in the center of the pan speeds cooking. Also, it's easier to cut! Try it.

After washing the dishes that night . . . I have a clean pan. I reach into the refrigerator, take out the already prepared meat loaf, stuff it into the clean angel food cake pan and put it in the freezing compartment.

As soon as the meat mixture is frozen, I take the pan and turn it upside down under the hot-water faucet, letting the hot water run over the bottom of the pan. The block of frozen meat loaf comes loose from the pan.

Then I tear a piece of foil off and lay it on the drainboard. I place the angel food cake pan upside down on the foil and in a few minutes the beautiful ring of meat drops onto the foil. I remove the pan, fold the foil over the loaf and place it in the freezer again.

When ready to bake this meat loaf, I can place it back in the same pan or bake it in a skillet. In the meantime, I have that angel food cake pan if I need it for something else.

From New York: "Here's one for the girls to try: Add one package of onion soup to your **meat loaves** and some canned evaporated milk. Great!"

SLICE AND ICE

From Ohio: "Did you know that you can freeze **meat** slices on a cookie sheet and then place them in a plastic bag in the freezer, and they will not stick together?

"It works just like hamburger patties. I froze sliced cooked ham and roast beef this way, and also raw, *separated* bacon slices! No sticking at all."

MEATBALLS—QUICKER BY THE DOZEN

From Louisiana: "I hate to brown tiny **meatballs!** They seem to take ages. I was inspired one day to invent an easy, smokeless method. I made the meatballs and placed them on an ungreased, foil-covered cookie sheet. The meat itself will grease the foil on the cookie pan. I put them under the broiler for ten or fifteen minutes until they browned on one side. I then turned them over and browned them on the other side.

"You can proceed to cook them in any way. The balls retain their shape far better, and less handling is necessary.

"Another thing: When you make these little tid bits— whether for parties or for your good old spaghetti—you can make lots of them . . . they can be frozen and used later for many things."

GROWING PAINS

From Iowa: "As my family started to grow and medicines began to accumulate, the crowded **medicine chest** would not hold everything. I set aside a spacious high shelf in the bathroom linen closet for medicines. A shallow open box containing all of 'his' or 'her' prescriptions was designated for each member of the family with an extra family box containing general medicines, such as for first-aid treatment.

"Not a single tube, bottle or jar gets overturned or misplaced, and, wonder of wonders, the shelf has a neat appearance!

"On the inside of our closet door I have attached a printed

sheet of first-aid facts! This includes doctors' telephone numbers, plus other medical information."

For the small tubes of ointment, etc., which clutter up a **medicine cabinet** so easily, use a small plastic bowl or dish such as is used for leftovers in the refrigerator. The dish takes up less space and the cabinet looks better organized.

MURDER THAT MILDEW!

A homemaker writes: "Please tell us how to get the **mildew** and mold out of the grout between the ceramic tiles in our bathrooms and shower."

Mildew is a growth.

Household bleach removes the *color* of the mildew but does not kill the fungus . . . so I am told by a very reputable chemist in a big laboratory.

Ammonia will kill the fungus but the two procedures should be done *separately*. Here's how:

First use plain household bleach. Use a sponge or old brush.

Leave this on the *ceramic* tiles until it dries; a few hours or even overnight won't hurt.

Then rinse with clear water.

Dip a cloth in household ammonia (I hold my nose and use it straight, but you can dilute it) and scour the tiles. The ammonia will help kill the tiny spores which are there, even if you can't see them. *Let this dry.*

Most people just bleach the grout and the mildew grows right back and they wonder why. . . . That spore has to be killed! Since we can't shoot 'em with buckshot, why not use something less dangerous, like ammonia?

Now, if you would like to help prevent soap film and accumulation from forming again on your tile, take an old washrag, dip it in some plain kerosene, wring it out and wipe the tiles after they are completely dry.

This will not only give the tile a sheen, but soap suds and water will "bead" and *run off.*

The kerosene odor will soon leave. I do this once every week or so in our bath. Use *only* on the walls. It might be too slippery to be used on the floor.

SEE "RED"—AND PULL!

From Pennsylvania: "We bought a house that has a light with a pull chain over the bathroom **mirror.** For two years I cleaned this mirror daily because all of the family reached up, grabbed the chain, and after it was pulled, it 'flopped' all over the mirror, causing fingerprints and other marks.

"I went to the dime store and bought a curtain pull. These are ordinarily used on blinds, but anyone could put anything that is weighted on the bottom of this pull chain.

"I bought a red curtain pull. The reason I did this was so that when my family goes to the bathroom—and they are usually absentminded—they will see 'red' and will pull on this immediately instead of reaching up on the mirror where they leave their fingerprints.

"I find that this not only eliminated cleaning the mirror every day, but the pull holds the string straight and prevents scratching as well."

LETTING OFF STEAM

Did you know that bathroom **mirrors** will not steam up if you run a little soap-type shaving cream on the mirror and then rub the cream off with a towel? Toilet tissue may be better to use, because it doesn't streak the way a towel sometimes does.

A little glycerine wiped on bathroom **mirrors and windows** and buffed with a soft cloth will keep them from steaming up, too.

DO IT WITH MIRRORS

From Pennsylvania: "I had a hard time getting my eight-year-old to brush his teeth until I put a small **mirror** over the sink just for him. Now he brushes his teeth without coaxing.

"The medicine-chest mirror (which is adult height) was much too high for him, but now that he can see what he's doing, he's more interested in his appearance. I bought a small mirror about nine by twelve inches with clamps at the top and it rests on the sink. This way we can raise the height of the mirror as he grows taller."

BUILDING YOUR NEST EGG

A letter from local neighbors: "At our coffee klatch this morning we discussed the fact that none of us can *save!*

"Our husbands all have a good income they think—and we agree with them. But even though we all try, we cannot come up with an answer to the question of how to save **money.**

"I have been married for twelve years and we have less than three hundred dollars in the bank for emergencies. We also have no savings. Yes, we live day-to-day.

"It would be so wonderful if you could teach us how to save. We all worry, What if that catastrophe should come? For example, we discussed automobile accidents, sicknesses, hospital bills, pregnancies and immediate necessities.

"It is bad enough when your refrigerator conks out. Much worse, the thought of our washing machine needing the skill of a repairman! We must learn to save."

Do you know that for many generations *experts* have been working on this subject, and they give you a book and tell you how to balance the budget and how to live on your income?

Saving is just like life. It becomes a habit! But what a beautiful habit to form!

It's nice to know that you have a nest egg set aside in case of trouble, but how much nicer it is to know you have that little nest egg just to give you a sense of security.

Here's the way I save:

I know that this is not the only answer and I don't believe you will find it in any book. Before I spend a dollar—especially on something that is not food or a necessity—I say to *myself,* "Now this costs *one dollar.* We *save 10 percent* of our income, so my husband has to make ten dollars in order for me to spend this one dollar. Now, *is this item* worth my husband working so many hours to make that *ten dollars* or *can I do without it?*"

When you start to think of money in terms of hours of labor, then you will begin to save.

Many people with savings accounts tell me (and I believe it) that they pay their "savings bill" first! If you would consider your monthly or weekly savings quota as a *bill* and pay it first, and *then* budget the rest of your money, you will find that you will soon have that nice little backlog. Remember that back in the old days, you could not keep warm unless you had logs to burn!

When you get enough surplus built up in your savings account, you can pay cash for things and save the interest.

Ladies, I cannot tell you how to save. All I can do is tell you *how to spend*. Sensible spending, conservative buying and careful budgeting is the best answer I have.

KEEP IT LIGHT

When purchasing a **mop,** buy the *lightest weight* possible. Here's why:

Sometimes expensive string mops are heavy. They have a lot more strings, longer strings, last longer, etc. But for a poor little housewife with a tired back, aching feet and a bunch of kids . . . lifting that heavy mop it quite unnecessary.

Test this yourself:

Buy a cheap mop, *wet it thoroughly* and compare it with an expensive, heavy string mop and see which weighs the most! One will outweigh the other, two- or three-to-one. Just who is going to shove, push and pull it around? *You!* And don't forget that the heavy, thick mops are harder to wash, harder to clean and rinse. Take longer to dry, also.

It's much better (and will save lots of energy) if you will buy a small, lightweight mop (and broom, too, for that matter).

I am well aware that the expensive mop might last longer, but if you compare the price, you will find that you can buy two cheaper mops or brooms that weigh much less, for about the same price as a heavy one. Just buy them *twice as often!*

It eventually comes out to the same cost, money-wise. I figure our energy sometimes is worth a lot more than something which lasts a long time. My answer is to buy lighter-weight mops and brooms and save our backs.

n

FILING THE FILE

For women who use emery boards and want to save: Here's a tip when the edges wear down. Take your scissors and trim the emery board off an eighth of an inch along the edge. (It sharpens your scissors, too!)

By doing this, the **nail** file can be used over and over until there's none left.

"SHOOT" THE WORKS

Did you ever try dropping several pellets of BB shot into your **nail polish** bottle? Each time you use the polish, shake well and the polish is easily, quickly and thoroughly mixed. This is especially good for the frosted types of polishes. It also raises the level of the polish so that the brush always reaches it.

NAILING DOWN THE HABIT

To break the habit of **nail-biting:** Rub the nails along a bar of soap and then rinse them.

Just enough soap will remain under the child's nails to make the whole process unpleasant.

NEEDLE POINTERS

From California: "When my sewing machine **needles** start pulling thread, I sharpen them on an emery. One can usually find a hook on the end of a needle which will file off easily. I find this makes them as good as new. A whetstone is also good for this."

To remove rust from a **needle,** push it through a piece of flannel saturated with machine oil. Or if it's very rusty, push it through a soap-filled steel wool pad a few times.

From Delaware: "As the result of losing a **needle** which I had stuck in the hole of a spool of thread, I took an inch of cellophane tape and stuck it over the hole of the spool. Then I stuck the needle through the tape. It's always there! The stickiness of the tape holds the needle in place."

Don't throw away those old lipstick containers. Those empty tubes can be used for holding **needles** and so forth.

Before washing them, dig out the remaining lipstick. The best way to do this is to put the tube in the freezing compartment of your refrigerator. Then when it's frozen, when you stick a paring knife in the remaining portion, the lipstick will pop out!

After this, wash the tube thoroughly in hot suds and let it drain dry.

Then all you have to do is place all of those straight pins in it and put it in your sewing box.

NEWLYWEDS

Many of you have just gone into orbit! Your eyes are full of enthusiasm and your hearts are full of love. You're **newlyweds.** Wonderful!

Your hands are soft and smooth and your friends have given you precious silver and crystal and beautiful, thick bath towels. Great! Take care of that silver and crystal, and your beautiful bath towels, because a few years from now you are going to have to buy cheaper ones or look for sales. You also will have to look at diapers, formulas, bills and the price of groceries.

Your mother has been through all this. Some of you have never realized it before. We look at Mother as if she were from another planet. Well, she didn't have frozen foods and TV when she was your age. But she had problems—and solved them.

Ask your mother for some tips. She'll love it!

And . . . read! Read everything you can. Learn.

I am going to give you a few hints, not advice. (The greatest advice I ever had was from a neighbor before I was married. She said: "Heloise, the best advice I can give you is not to take any advice that anyone gives to you.")

But listen to what people say. Then decide whether you can make use of their experience. Just because people tell you how to clean silver doesn't mean you *have* to clean it that way.

After you return from your honeymoon, keep those stars in your eyes. But don't work yourself to death to do it!

When your husband goes off to work, get the most important things done first. Make the bed, do your dishes, empty the ash trays and hang the bath towels straight.

As soon as he walks out the door, fill your kitchen sink with all your dirty dishes and put in some detergent, then turn the hot-water faucet on until the dishes are covered. Forget them for a while. (Never put your hands in hot water if you can help it. Mother didn't know this in her day.)

Immediately go into the bedroom and make the bed.

Next, go back and have that second cup of coffee or tea. Read the paper. Your dishes are soaking, your beds are made and you aren't in too bad shape even if your mother-in-law drops in.

After that cup of coffee, your dishwater should be cold. Go back and pull the plug out of the sink and let the water drain. Then, and only then, rinse your dishes under the faucet and put them in that dish drainer. You have saved energy, time and your hands.

Now what to do with the laundry and ironing? Don't worry about it. Just get it done. For the rest of your life, you will have it. And the longer you are married, the more laundry you will have.

Don't try to be a perfectionist. Don't do the laundry every Monday, ironing on Tuesday, etc., as our mothers did. Do it when you're in the mood. If it's Saturday . . . fine! Who cares? As long as you have clean clothes.

But keep ahead. The days you have energy and feel good— that's when to clean closets, cook, bake and wash and iron. You'll do the work twice as fast!

I suggest that you newlyweds buy a few inexpensive musts before you spend your money on flat silver, good dishes or even a new dress.

Buy a carpet sweeper, a feather duster, and begin saving for a deep freeze.

The carpet sweeper is wonderful for the days when you have to get "the middle" clean in a hurry. When you are low on energy, an old feather duster is wonderful. Some day you will get a phone call from husband (that's the *doll* you married a few months ago, remember?) and he will say, "I'm bringing a friend home" or "Mother is dropping by tonight."

Don't let this upset you. Just get that carpet sweeper out and that old feather duster and "Hit Heloise's Middle!" Your home will be neat.

And, girls, remember that never yet has my husband or a guest lifted up a bedspread to see if I had dusted under the bed. Nor has any guest moved a piece of furniture to see if I had cleaned behind it! These are necessary chores. That's for sure. But don't pull your insides out trying to do them every day. Do them when necessary.

Another thing—don't save your very best silver, dishes and linen only for company. There will *never* be anyone in your home any better or more deserving than your husband. Let him enjoy the best. He deserves it. And so do you. Use the best daily. The graveyards are full of women who saved all of their beautiful things hoping that *THE* day would come. *The* day never comes. *The* day is here today. Use it, enjoy it and make the most of it. This is living.

ONION HEAD

From a reader: "I always leave the 'head' on one end of an **onion** when I grate it and use this as a handle. That way I save my fingernails.

"When onion is grated down near to the end just discard the rest. No waste really, because this part is usually cut off and thrown away."

KNOW YOUR ONIONS!

Dare you to try this trick from a lady in New York: "I cannot stand the odor of paint. Know what I do? I chop up a big bowl of **onions** and set it on the floor in each room when I am painting. I take a spoon and turn them from time to time. This way I get the aroma of onions instead of the paint odor."

FOR TOP-HEAVY FIGURINES

From California: "We all love those pottery **ornaments,** but they do tip over and break sometimes, don't they?

"Fill them about one-third full of sand, put some masking tape over the hole, and they won't be top-heavy any more. Sometimes I fill them nearly full of sand and they are heavy enough to use as bookends."

KNEE ACTION

For mothers with toddlers who tear their **overalls** in the knee section: You can buy iron-on tape at the dime store in assorted colors and cut it into the shape of an elephant, rabbit, etc., and iron over the worn spot on the outside of the garment.

This is most intriguing, not only to the child himself but to those who see him later. It works on any kind of garment, including blue jeans.

For everyday overalls, blue jean "patches" are the best, especially when the child is crawling on the floor.

NO MESSES FOR THE MISSUS!

From Philadelphia: "Putting the lid back on a half-used can of **paint** can be pretty messy.

"Here is a trick I learned from my mother. After opening a new can of paint, take a hammer and a large nail and punch five or six holes in the lid-retaining groove. That's all there is to it!

"When you dip the brush in the paint and then wipe it against the side of the can rim, the paint fills the groove as it always does. But with the holes, it runs right back into the can.

"When you replace the lid, the paint doesn't 'squish' out and you save the paint, too. The lid seals the nail holes and the can is still airtight!"

From Honolulu: "When I am **painting,** I always stretch a *heavy* rubber band or cord across the open top of my paint can. This allows for a place to wipe the brush gently each time I dip for paint, and so it keeps the paint from dripping down the side of my small paint can."

From Kentucky: "I suggest that when you're getting ready to **paint** and pouring paint from a can, you use a plastic milk carton which has been cut down to an appropriate size with a knife. This sure saves washing out another container and it can be thrown away later. I have found that the plastic on the inside of the milk carton will allow all the paint to be poured back into the original can."

From Nevada: "When **painting,** you will find that a paper plate is useful as a tray for the paint can. It is also a convenient place to put the brush.

"When painting woodwork, I coat the door knobs, locks and latches with petroleum jelly so the paint can be wiped off easily if it splashes on these surfaces."

WHEN YOU'RE AIMING HIGH

From Connecticut: "If you put on a rubber glove when you **paint** ceilings and turn the cuff of the glove back an inch or so, the cuff will catch all the drippings!

"This is good for washing ceilings, too. The water just seems to drip, drip, and the cuff catches all the water that usually runs down your arm.

"When the cuff is full of water, turn your hand down over the bucket and all the water will flow back into the bucket."

From a man in New York: "We own a chain of apartments. Being the husband, I am elected to do all the **paint** jobs.

"I use a paint roller. And do you know what I have found? It is the best thing for painting a ceiling as well as walls.

"I use swim goggles. When I'm painting a ceiling and the goggles get spattered so much that I cannot see, I just wipe them off with kerosene!"

PAINTING POINTERS

From Montreal: "I roll on **paint** and then stroke with a brush. This will use a little more paint, but the time saved is worth it. It's terrific! I use this method on cupboards in the kitchen. The necessity of a good brush cannot be overemphasized—do take care of it."

From Florida: "For professional results when **painting** with enamel, take a putty knife or any other knife and skim off the film. Do not stir this film. Then take a worn nylon stocking and strain your paint. Stir the paint and continue as usual."

From Arizona: "When I am **painting** a ceiling or anything that requires the brush to be higher than my hand, I wrap a piece of old cloth around the top of the handle. This keeps the paint from running down the handle and getting on my hands and eventually running down my arm."

From Maine: "When **painting** anything, such as the side of your house or a piece of furniture, take a plastic bag of the kind vegetables come in and cut the bottom out.

"Put one bag on each forearm and then put rubber bands on either end of the bag, and your arms will stay paint-free while you are getting the job done! Saves all the drips, cleaning spots off arms, etc."

YOU'LL BE GLAD YOU DID

From Montana: "When my neighbor **paints** with a roller, she puts a large plastic or paper bag over her roller pan before putting the paint in the pan, and when she is through painting she just pulls the bag off and her pan is clean."

From South Carolina: "When you've started **painting** and you are interrupted but plan on getting back to your painting

in an hour or so, wrap your brushes or your roller in a piece of plastic wrap.

"I have left brushes and rollers wrapped overnight and they were still just as moist and nice as they were when I stopped painting. Saves a lot of time and fuss."

ONE COAT WILL DO

A professional house painter in New Jersey sent this tip: "Will you please tell your readers that it is far better to **paint** the outside trim or walls of a house once every two years with one coat of paint than to use two coats of paint at any one time? This gives the paint a chance to 'season.'

"Many people think that the heavier the paint, the better. Not so. Thin the paint slightly until the brush does not 'pull' and leave streaks.

"And when we painters get ready to paint the outside, we throw an old tarpaulin with a rope tied to each end over the shrubs and stake the ends of the rope to the ground. This holds the shrubs away from the sides of the house but does not damage them. An old sheet or shower curtain could be used instead of tarpaulin."

BE A SPOT SPOTTER

From Los Angeles: "Here's a hint for those who **paint** their own rooms—whether they use roll-on paint or any other type:

"Save those old two-ounce and four-ounce medicine bottles.

When you're through painting that living room, bedroom, bathroom, etc., pour a medicine bottle full of the paint used in each room. Label it quickly! Use thick nail polish to label the bottle. If you don't use nail polish, take adhesive tape and stick it on the bottle and then take your ball point pen and label which room it is for. Keep these bottles on a convenient storage shelf.

"Then, when a chair brushes against the wall, a child marks on it, a friend or foe leaves a handprint, or you happen to hit it with your mop, go to the shelf immediately and pick up the bottle of paint labeled for that particular room. Shake the bottle and then dab a piece of cotton on the end as if you were going to apply mercurochrome to an injury. Use the wet cotton to dab the mark generously, fluttering and feathering out to the edge of the spot. It covers!

"With a nine-room house and six kids, I have been saved many frustrations by doing this. My house always looks as if it had just been newly painted.

"Since I have so many little ones, I use this same method around the door handles where the kids leave their print marks. I have found that I can take one wad of cotton and, instead of dabbing it on real heavy marks, I can wipe it gently around the doorknobs and light switches, eliminating all of the dirty marks on my painted woodwork.

"I have also found that I can use white shoe polish applied to a piece of cotton to 'spot' my white walls."

LET'S FACE IT!

An old remedy to remove **paint** from your hands, face and so forth: After you have finished painting, take a small piece of butter or a cloth dipped in baby oil and rub it on your hands, face, legs or whatever the paint has splattered.

Rub it in well and wipe it off. Then wash with soap and water.

It is so much better for your skin than turpentine or other paint remover.

From South Carolina: "For years I have been **painting** ceilings in my home with a roller and I always end up with a lovely crop of white 'freckles.'

"Enamel paint (which I always use in the kitchen and bath) is very hard to remove. It usually takes some kind of cleaning solution, and they are not particularly good for the face.

"Before you start to paint, cover your face and neck liberally with cold cream. When you are through painting, just wipe your face with a facial tissue and all your ugly 'paint freckles' are gone!

"Needless to say, it's a good idea to cover your hair and wear an old, long-sleeved shirt."

LESS PATCH WORK

From Missouri: "When applying the iron-on **patches** to any garment—such as the worn-out knees on little boys' slacks—I find it is helpful to place a piece of aluminum foil under the garment before ironing on the patch.

"The foil not only concentrates the heat but also eliminates any tendency of the patch to stick to the ironing board! The foil may be peeled off. This saves sticky damage to your cover."

THIS POCKET-PICKING IS NO CRIME!

For those of you who have men's and boys' cotton wash trousers with dirty **pockets** that simply will not come clean, pouring ammonia full strength on the pocket and lining and scrubbing with a vegetable brush works wonders.

I let mine sit about twenty minutes and then wash them in the machine. This removes all of the stains caused by silver, (ah, money!) and the accumulated dirt from hand perspiration.

Now, don't run and gather all of your husband's trousers and try them all at once. He might not stand the shock. I do suggest that you try one pair and see how you come out.

Incidentally, boys' wash pants did extremely well with this treatment.

FITTING THE PATTERN

From Connecticut: "I sew a great deal, and I have found that the pieces of a **pattern** will go back into an envelope more neatly if they are ironed and then folded a little smaller than the original crease and envelope. I have heard many people complain about being unable to fit patterns back into the envelopes—can't quite understand it!"

Did you ever try taping a paper dress **pattern** to your material instead of pinning it? You can cut right through the tape and don't have to be bothered removing pins!

PET IDEAS

If you are forever retrieving your **pet's** favorite ball from under the furniture, tie it inside an old nylon stocking. It will still bounce and roll—but only so far—and the stocking gives him something to swing the ball by.

From New York: "After years of dog feeding, I have found that it's a good idea to open both ends of the can of dog food, leaving the tops *stuck* to the food. *Push* the food through one end of the can into the dog bowl. If the dog cannot eat a whole can at one feeding, simply take a knife and cut off what he can eat and replace the ends of the can. This saves mess and prevents waste of food. Or instead of using a knife, why not use the lid from one end of the can to cut the dog food?"

From Ohio: "Canned dog food can be kept moist after opening by being capped with a standard-sized fruit-jar lid! Put the lid in upside down and place the can back in the refrigerator. Keeps fresh for at least two days."

From New Jersey: "We have a dog and have discovered something which has proved invaluable to us. We cut the leather handstrap off his leash and substituted his outgrown leather collar (the buckle kind). If we're walking our dog and must stop in a grocery store or such where dogs aren't allowed, we simply buckle the leash around anything handy until we return."

From Oregon: "When you're traveling in the car with **pets,** fill a plastic bottle with water each morning before starting the day's journey. The pets can have fresh water while you are driving without your wasting time to look for water on the way. Take along a small bowl, pour out a few ounces of the water at a time and let the pet lap away."

SAVE YOUR SCENTS!

From a friend and housewife: "Here is a tip I would like to share with my friends and housewives. When that good bottle of **perfume** is empty and not another drop can be gotten out of it, don't throw it away."

"I always remove the top and set the bottle in my laundry hamper. This way, the fragrance of the perfume evaporates from the bottle and makes a heavenly aroma in your clothes hamper."

MORE PING, LESS PONG

To take dents out of **ping-pong balls,** you can drop them in boiling water, turn them occasionally, and in a few minutes they will be as good as new.

USE BAKING SODA ON PLASTIC WARE

Please do not clean **plastic ware** with steel wool. This only ruins the finish.

The manufacturers of these plastic dishes write to me that even scouring powders and bleaches will ruin them. Once the finish has been removed there is nothing you can do. They suggest using only baking soda or a special product made for this purpose.

To use baking soda, you dip a damp cloth into regular soda and polish as if you were cleaning silver.

SUNLIGHT HARMS FOAM RUBBER

We have had so many complaints from folks who have foam rubber **pillows** which need to be washed! Some sweet gentleman who *knows* (and is with one of the biggest foam manufacturers in America) wrote the following to help us:

"Foam rubber pillows should never be hung in the sunlight because the ultraviolet rays in sunlight are enemies of foam rubber and cause it to crumble.

"Actually, since foam rubber itself has no odor, this problem is very seldom encountered. However, the foam rubber can pick up odors from hair oils, babies, etc. When this happens, the best thing to do is to wash the pillow by hand in lukewarm water, with a mild soap. Excess water should be squeezed out. Then let the pillow or other article dry in a cool place, *out of direct sunlight*. And remember—foam rubber should *never* be dried in an automatic drier.

"Some people may not have genuine foam rubber, but instead have pillows of urethane foam, a synthetic plastic substitute for foam rubber. This product sometimes has an unpleasant, chemical-like odor. In any case, sunlight is also damaging to urethane, making it age prematurely and turn a rather ugly yellow."

FRESHEN UP PILLOWCASES

From New York: "I have found that **pillowcases** and linens become musty between washings and ironings after they sit on the shelf a while waiting to be used.

"Recently, I sprayed my wet pillowcases with a healthy dose of non-toxic room air freshener, then put them in the drier. I now have the sweetest smelling pillowcases anyone could ask for."

PLAYTIME PILLOWS

If you have children in your home who watch TV and you would like to save your favorite toss **pillows** (and also your peace of mind), try this:

Most of us have old chenille bedspreads with some use still in them. Make covers from the good parts for the pillows. Make them so they will slip on and off easily.

These washable covers protect the pretty pillows and the youngsters can put them on the floor to sit on, or even play train with them.

Y NOT?

From a pie-loving teen-ager: "When you're serving a **pie** and you want to cut it into five equal pieces, cut a "Y" in the pie and then cut the two large pieces in half. You will then have five pieces exactly the same size."

BE A CUT-UP!

From a reader who likes **pizza:** "Cutting pizza with a knife was always a chore for me. I solved that little ol' problem by learning to use a pair of kitchen scissors for this job. Works wonders. Quick, clean and sharp without cutting your pan (or foil if you use foil to line the pan before baking)."

CORNBALL CAPERS

From Idaho: "I wonder how many people use bacon grease to add a special zest to **popcorn?**

"Just substitute the bacon grease for the cooking oil and you are in for a delicious surprise!"

From New Jersey: "You can wash empty milk cartons and use them as **popcorn** boxes.

"These cartons may be filled with popcorn and taken to drive-in movies or used at home.

"Half-gallon cartons may be used for adults and the pint or quart size for children.

"Just cut off the carton at the top until you have the proper size for each person.

"These may be thrown away, or washed and saved for use another time."

From Colorado: "When I make **popcorn** balls, I use a small lollipop on which to form the balls! The children and the grownups have a handle to hold while eating the popcorn ball, and a candy treat when the popcorn is gone!"

WHEN A POTATO "LOOKS" AT YOU—ACT!

We all buy **potatoes.** Baking potatoes, salad potatoes or new potatoes.

I have found out that potatoes do grow "eyes."

I have also found out—after experimenting for years with all kinds of potatoes—that when a potato grows an "eye," the potato starts to shrivel. This means the potato shrinks and the outside skin gets old . . . just like people!

When you see a potato growing that "eye" and looking up at you, take a knife or your fingernail and pop that growth off. The potato will not shrivel and get pithy as quickly as it would if you left the "eye" growing.

MEALS IN MINUTES

From Massachusetts: "I have four children, all hearty eaters, so I must serve **potatoes**—a lot and often.

"I buy ten pounds at a time, and after I set aside enough for one meal of mashed potatoes, I boil the rest with their jackets on. After they are cool, I store them in the refrigerator.

"I also boil eggs at the same time. With these two very basic foods cooked and ready for imaginative use, my quick menu possibilities are endless.

"I have reduced the time element in preparing potato salad, cheese and potato casserole, home fries, deviled eggs, etc."

SHAKE-DRY POTATOES

From Rhode Island: "I use boiled **potato** water in my gravies for a finer flavor. And, speaking of potatoes, after you pour off the water, place the saucepan over a low heat and shake the potatoes once or twice. This keeps them from sticking and they are ready to serve. They seem whiter and are dry and fluffy. I do this whether I serve them as is or mash them. To mash them and keep them hot, add milk and butter, heat on low heat until butter is melted, then beat with electric mixer."

FOILED AGAIN!

For years I have used rubber **powder puffs.** I have always carried one in an empty plastic compact while the puff is still damp.

I find that if I don't use it often enough, it starts smelling!

Then, a few years ago, I found out that the puffs won't smell if you carry them in waxed paper sandwich bags. The great thing about this is that the dampness does not come through the lining into your purse, yet the sandwich bag lets just enough of the moisture escape so that the puff doesn't smell.

When my husband saw me take my foam rubber powder puff from my worn, crumpled sandwich bag one day, he said, "Why don't you wrap it in a piece of foil?" Immediately he returned with a piece of foil, just a little larger than the powder puff itself. Now, after I apply my cake make-up, all I have to do is take the damp sponge, fold it in half, or roll it in the foil. Personally, I like to roll the sponge up and then put it in the foil because it stays damp longer. Also it doesn't take up as much room in my purse.

Gals, all of you who use cake make-up, skip into that kitchen, unroll that piece of foil, and lay it on your make-up table. In the morning when you do your face—this is especially for working girls—roll your sponge-type puff and put it in your little piece of foil and twist both ends.

You will find that this will last at least forty-eight hours. You will have no mess in your purse. It is easily seen for quick make-up jobs. But, best of all, it never has an odor.

QUILTED QUANDARIES

Do you mothers have trouble keeping the bottom end of **quilts** and blankets tucked in at night?

Take the good part of a worn-out sheet and baste it along the bottom of blankets, etc., in the center part of the blanket, just about the width of the mattress, but not quite.

Leave a nice large piece and tuck it under the mattress itself, and your bed-making will be a breeze.

You will not need to remove the quilt even to change the sheets, as the quilt can rest on the floor when turned back. It is then all ready to be brought back up smoothly over the bed again after the sheets have been changed.

From New York: "When my boys were small, I took the good parts of my worn contour sheets, the unworn part is usually along the sides of a sheet, or perhaps the end if you have twin beds, and I cut off the good contour sections. These I sewed to the bottoms of their **quilts.** They made the quilts contour on one end so they would slip over the bottoms of the mattresses. Keeps the quilts from sliding off the bed, and it's also easier to make the bed."

From Nebraska: "To hold the cover for **quilts,** blankets and comforters in place, all you need do is sew buttons on the blanket or comforter and make buttonholes to match on the sheet or cover. This should hold it sufficiently in place.

"In my native Germany this practice is quite common. The edge of the sheet that is folded over often has fancy embroidery."

COMFORTING THOUGHTS

From Washington, D.C.: "After chasing them for years, I finally found the answer to satin **quilts and comforters** that slip off the bed.

"I sewed a piece of muslin across the bottom of the comforter, nearly as wide as the cover itself. I now just tuck the piece of muslin under the mattress. Result . . . no chasing!"

From Pennsylvania: "To keep a satin **quilt or comforter** on the bed, I tack a small sheet or flannel blanket on the back of the quilt. It works fine!"

From Maine: "I keep my rayon satin **quilt** on the bed by covering it with ten yards of printed material. This costs only about forty-nine cents a yard.

"I tear this ten yards of material in half, which leaves me with two five-yard pieces. I then sew these two lengths together along the selvage. Fold this in half. Sew up both sides, forming a pillowcase-type sack. On the open end, sew buttons and buttonholes. (Snap or other type fasteners could be used.)

"Insert your satin comforter in this cover. When you put it on the bed, turn the buttons and buttonholes toward the bottom of the bed.

"Result? A comforter that never slips and a cover that may be removed in a jiffy for laundering."

P.S. These comforter or quilt covers may be store-bought.

r

CUTTING DOWN

From Cleveland: "Most women use **razors**. We are the saving type and like to use the blades for weeks, and I have found that if I keep my razor in a little jar of alcohol in the medicine cabinet, it doesn't rust and the blade lasts for ages.

"The alcohol also acts as an antiseptic. I just put the razor in the alcohol (naturally, blade end down), and even the oil accumulated between the razor and blade disappears."

KEEPING THE RECORDS STRAIGHT

For pre-school children who have their own **records** and phonographs, in order to help them identify the various tunes, cut out pictures of related subjects . . . a farmer for "Farmer in the Dell," a pirate ship for "Treasure Island," and so forth . . . and paste these pictures in the center of the record.

If some of your phonograph **records** have warped, try this: Take two sheets of glass (these can be removed from any pictures in the house, providing you put them back later!) and place a record between them. Put it on a flat surface and lay it in the sun one day.

After sundown and before dew sets in, remove the record and you will find it straight. This idea came from a company that makes records, and I have tried it and it works!

AN HOUR A DAY—JUST FOR YOU

Mothers and wives have hard lives, but it needn't be so.

Know what I think is the matter? We don't ever **relax**. We work too hard.

You think you owe it to your husband and children, but you owe something to yourself, too.

How's about settling for just one hour for yourself once in a while? It might make a new woman of you.

And don't feel guilty about a measly little hour. Enjoy it. Nobody deserves it more than you do.

Spend that hour taking a nice hot bath and putting plenty of face cream on your face. While you are in the tub give yourself a pedicure. Have a nice long soak.

You and your neighbor could agree to baby-sit for each other once a week, if only for an hour. And while your darlings are gone, utilize that hour spoiling yourself. If you do nothing but prop your feet up in a chair and stare at the ceiling . . . at least do that.

Don't share these few golden hours with a neighbor or friend. Then it becomes business again.

Don't shop. Do something horrible—just relax!

Typical letters from tired mothers all read the same: Alarm goes off in the morning . . . Yawn . . . Sigh . . . Go to kitchen in a sleepy daze . . . Plug in coffee pot . . . Get paper . . . Glance at headlines . . . Pick up skillet . . . Throw bacon in . . . Grab eggs . . . Butter toast . . . Pour coffee, take a sip . . . Wake up family . . . Yell at kids . . . Feed the brood . . . Kiss husband good-bye . . . Comb kids' hair (yell at 'em again) . . . Tell kids good-bye if they go to school . . . Turn around . . . Look at dirty dishes, laundry, unmade beds . . . Grab coffee pot and hope there's enough left . . . It happens in every household! Just laugh and quit fretting.

But try changing your routine. You won't be so bored, which makes you more tired.

For a change, take your first cup of coffee into your living room—*don't drink it in the kitchen*—and meditate alone for five minutes.

Eat in the dining room (instead of the breakfast room or the kitchen) once in a while. Then make the family carry their own dishes to the kitchen drainboard.

Try ironing in the living room or on a porch instead of the kitchen! You just might be surprised how much faster, more enjoyable, and less complicated ironing can be.

Instead of eating a peanut butter and jelly sandwich for lunch, why not a baked potato and hamburger, or a grilled cheese sandwich and a lettuce salad with dressing, served on your prettiest plate—and don't eat it in the kitchen! Prop up on the sofa or even in bed.

Remember, wives and mothers are irreplaceable!

So enjoy at least one hour a week for spoiling yourself. It's cheaper than tranquilizers and doctor bills.

SHRINK FIRST

From Iowa: "I have had trouble with **rickrack** shrinking more than the material until I found that the rickrack could be pre-shrunk before sewing it on the garment! All I do is just dip the card of rickrack in hot water and use a towel to remove excess moisture and let it dry on the card. It does not require ironing. Then apply as usual to the garment."

SOUNDPROOF ROCKING CHAIR

For those who have gotten into the habit of using that old **rocking chair** again—and gee, do *I* love it—I have found that noise, and marking and marring of floors, are eliminated when you glue some felt weather stripping on the bottom of the rockers. Weather stripping of the kind usually applied to doors and windows can be bought by the yard.

BE RUFFLED!

Those of you who want to make perfect gathering for the little **ruffles** that are so pretty: Set the sewing machine for the longest stitch, loosen the tension a bit, and then sew down the ruffle to be gathered.

Look at the bottom of the stitching and you will see the thread is very loose. All you have to do then is pull the loose thread and make the ruffle as loose or tight as you want.

BE A SWEEP-STAKES WINNER!

For those who have carpeted stairways . . . here's the answer to preserving **rugs**, energy, and keeping the carpeting clean.

If you have a tank-type vacuum cleaner, it will do a thorough job. Beginning at either the top or bottom of the stairway and using your *small* attachment—the one for cleaning upholstery—you can get into every nook and corner. However, this takes so much energy and moving of the tank that I do not do it often.

Another way is to use a *dampened* broom. I do this by making a weak solution of neutral detergent and dipping the broom in it, hitting it against the side of the pail so that it is not too wet, and then sweeping the entire carpet from top to bottom.

Then, beginning at the *bottom* step, use the vacuum attachment to suck up any moisture and soil that comes loose, working until you reach the top step.

I am sure that not many women realize it, but the riser (the carpet which lies on the edge of the step and is seldom walked on) also accumulates dust. This should be vacuumed once in a while also.

In between thorough cleanings, I have found a miniature carpet sweeper—which can be purchased in children's toy departments—was the answer to all of my troubles. This little carpet sweeper is a toy. But it works! It is so narrow that it fits on each step with no effort, and the brush still goes around because all wheels of the carpet sweeper stay on the steps. It is easily emptied because it is so small that it fits over any wastebasket, and, best of all, its light weight saves energy.

It would pay any homemaker to purchase one of these toy miniature carpet sweepers. They are quite useful for small spot cleaning up, such as where an ashtray has spilled.

FIT FOR A QUEEN

It is becoming quite popular to carpet bathrooms with cotton carpeting, and it is so pretty. Here is a hint that will prevent a big heartache:

Before you cut the rug to fit your bathroom (be sure to buy the carpeting *at least* six inches longer than your bathroom measures), have the whole piece of carpeting washed and dried so that it will do all of its shrinking before it is cut to fit.

There have been people who have cut their rug to fit, and after washing, it pulled away from the walls about two inches.

A BRUSH WITH THE FUZZ

From Connecticut: "After my cotton bathroom rug was washed for the first time, it was full of fuzz and I thought it was ruined.

"My next-door neighbor told me that I had washed the rug improperly and now I know she was right. I would like to pass her instructions along.

"I know that it was not soap-free. You can use either a water softener or a half-cup of vinegar in the rinse water. In the drier, I found that it was best not to let the rug get completely dry, because this seems to shrink it. I then laid it out on a concrete floor and took a wire brush and brushed the fuzz in all directions. This gave me perfect results and it looked as good as new! After all, we women only splurge once in a while, and this is one splurge (a bathroom rug) that we don't go wild over every day!"

CARPET BAGGING

From Florida: "I shampoo my own rugs. I have found that I can tie little plastic bags on the legs of my furniture to prevent rust marks from forming on my carpet when it's wet. This is not as unsightly as other materials used to prevent permanent markings."

RUG RECIPES AND CARPET CAPERS

From Minneapolis: "I remove crushed spots on my **rugs** and carpets when rearranging my furniture by taking a damp washcloth—well wrung out—and laying it over the spot. I then *lightly* touch the cloth with a warm iron, thus causing enough steam to raise the pile. By using a plain vegetable brush to brush the nap lightly, the spots are gone."

From Los Angeles: "I have found out what to do with that toilet water someone gave me.

"I sprinkle a dash of toilet water on the bag of my vacuum cleaner. As I vacuum **rugs** and carpets, the odor penetrates the entire house. I find that this odor is most delightful!"

From Pennsylvania: "Those who have old **rugs** with worn fringe, do what I did! I took the scissors and whacked the fringe right off! Then I took some iron-on tape and, pulling the edge of the rug back, I ironed the little selvage that was left to the back of the rug.

"Now I don't have an old-fashioned rug any more, and the dirty fringe is gone. Such a pleasure to look at the rug, too."

From Ontario: "Don't laugh, but I've found a way to keep from moving heavy pieces of furniture when I vacuum my **rugs.**

"These have a 'toe' space that is not big enough to get any attachment under but plenty big enough to see under. Just take your vacuum to your piece of furniture and point the blower in at that little toe space!

"Then . . . stand by to vacuum up the dust as it comes rolling out at your feet! Sure cleans it out."

From a rug manufacturer: "All who keep complaining that scatter **rugs** lose the rubber backing after a few washings should be told that they are rotting the rubber by using *too hot water.*

"When you wash this type of rug, the water should never be over 105 degrees.

"When they are dried, the drier should be set at the lowest possible temperature. They should not be over-dried."

From Illinois: "When rubberized backing on throw **rugs** wears thin after several washings, the rugs tend to wrinkle up on the floor and become dangerously slippery.

"When I buy throw rugs, I like to get two of the same color and size. Then, when the backing wears thin, I sew them together—back to back!

"This gives me one nice thick rug in place of two miserable ones. I use the longest stitch on my sewing machine and sew right around the outside edge.

"The rug will then be heavy enough to stay in place and look good. It will surprise you by giving many years of additional wear.

"There is another advantage to this: When the rug gets dirty, flip it over and use the other side. This way it's twice as long between washings.

"If you have a throw rug which is quite large, it can be folded in half and sewn the same way."

From Honolulu: "I repaired a burn in my **rug.** The method worked beautifully and I can hardly tell where the burn was.

"I removed some 'fuzz' from the rug (this can be done either by shaving or pulling some out with tweezers) and rolled it in my hand until it was the shape of the cigarette burn.

"Then I put a good cement glue on the backing of the rug and put the roll of fuzz down in the burned spot and placed a piece of cleansing tissue over it . . . then placed a heavy book on top. This will cause the glue to dry very slowly and you will get good results."

From Vermont: "We had the most horrible old faded **rug** that you have ever seen. We couldn't afford to have it dyed, nor could we afford the price of a new one.

"I took the rug to the garage, rolled it out on the floor, and cleaned it thoroughly with the vacuum. Next, I mixed five packages of all-purpose dye according to the directions on the carton, except that I used half as much water as called for.

I then took a broom and dipped it in the pail of dye water and swept the rug. I swept in all directions to spread the dye evenly into all of the rug fibers.

"I left the rug in the garage for a week to be sure it had dried thoroughly before replacing it in the living room again. Each morning I would take the broom and sweep the rug again. This caused the nap to become fluffy. My rug is now rejuvenated—bright and colorful—and we are pleased with the results."

From Michigan: "For those who live in old, windy houses with drafts that come through the floors and seep up through the **rugs:**

"Pull the rug back and place plastic bags under it! This will block the drafts, keep the floor warm and save on fuel bills. Plastic can be bought in sheets for this purpose, too.

"Be sure the plastic is completely under the rug so that children or pets cannot get at it.

"By using this method, we saved our children many unnecessary colds last year from their playing on the floor."

And I can remember during the Depression (and way before central heating) when people would put newspapers under their rugs, not only to keep the house warm in winter and avoid drafts, but also to keep it cooler in summer. Newspapers also cushion the backs of rugs if you have no rug pads, and help prolong their life.

Wisdom from an expert: "As the technical director of a cleaning institute, I would like to give some advice about spots on **rugs:**

"The best time to remove a spot is immediately after it happens. Remove all the moisture you can from the carpet immediately. In 90 percent of the cases, the liquid stains can be removed by thorough blotting.

"Place blotting material—such as toweling—over the damaged spot and push hard with the fingers or press hard with the ball of your bare foot, changing the cloth from time to time, until no more moisture can be absorbed from the carpet.

"After this initial blotting put at least one-half inch of clean, dry tissue or a folded white towel on top of the spot and weight it down with heavy books. Leave it at least eight hours, and further moisture will be absorbed.

"Even if no other cleaning procedures are used, a large portion of the stain will be removed.

"A professional cleaner cannot remove certain spots because of chemical changes which have taken place before the rug reaches him. By using the above method, when the rug is professionally cleaned you will be less likely to have a spot show up."

From Oregon: "A friend of mine was visiting my home while I was cleaning a spot on my rug with carbon tetrachloride. She was shocked that I had found this easy method of cleaning and told me it was dangerous to use. Is this true? It seems like a good cleaner to me."

Possible death can result from using carbon tetrachloride as a cleaner. The American Medical Association and the National Institute of Rug Cleaning warn that, although it is a good solvent, it has a high toxicity and may be absorbed through the skin into the blood stream. It also has an anesthetic effect when inhaled and may affect organic tissues of the kidneys, heart and liver. Your friend was right—take her advice. If you ever *have* to use it, make sure the room is *well ventilated.*

From New York: "Please help me, Heloise. I am desperate! My husband would die if he ever found out how foolish I was.

"I made the mistake of putting my upright deep freezer in a bedroom on a beautiful expensive rug. I guess I just was not thinking, because when I defrosted the deep freezer some of the water ran down onto the legs. I have moved the deep freezer and my rug is ruined. It is solid rust. The legs have pressed into the rug and there is nothing I can do. I have put everything I know of on the stain.

"I also have some heavy club chairs with little metal castors on the legs. The casters have rusted my rug, too. I feel this was caused from the humidity in the air. I would appreciate any help you can give."

I hope I have the answer for you. Now, buy some liquid rust remover. It will cost about a dollar. Pour this on a terry cloth washrag and rub the spot. Rub thoroughly and briskly. I believe you will find that all the rust will be removed. *Before* doing anything, check your rug for color fastness. This is the caution that is on all bottles.

On some rugs that have badly impressed stains of rust, I have poured minute amounts of the rust remover directly on the rug itself. Do not use a brush. Be sure to use a piece of terry cloth. After the stain is completely removed, rinse the rug as usual. Be *sure* to place a white bath towel on top of it and weight it down with books until completely dry.

For those of you who have carpet sweepers, here is a little hint that will help get a cleaner **rug:**

If you turn the sweeper over and look on the bottom, you will see that it is full of lint and threads. I have found that if I take my scissors and "clip" all of the threads at intervals, they will easily pull out!

Another hint: If you also have a vacuum cleaner, run the end nozzle of the cleaner over the bottom of the sweeper after those threads are clipped. All the residue from the sweeper will be sucked out!

Now, here is the best of the bunch: The brush on carpet sweepers is removable. I wonder how many women have ever thought that it needs to be washed once in a while? I wash mine in nice detergent suds and rinse in vinegar water.

Put the brush in your kitchen window and let it dry thoroughly. Place back in your carpet sweeper and you will find that you not only have a cleaner carpet but also a "new" sweeper as well.

SANDY SOLUTIONS

From Arizona: "I put **sand** (from the beach or any place you can dig it up) in our car ash trays!

"Now it is a simple matter for the driver of the car to snuff out his cigarette, and no more still-smoking stubs to dig out!"

From Minnesota: "Save your paper milk cartons, rinse and fill them with ordinary **sand.** When snowy or icy conditions exist, you then have a handy supply of sand to sprinkle on sidewalks and driveways.

"We also keep a few of the milk cartons filled with sand in the back of the car for those slick parking spots."

BUILD YOUR OWN SANDBOX

If father is slow to build a **sandbox** for the "small fry," go to a tire dealer and ask him for an old tractor-type tire. It is the nicest sandbox ever, and has a seat all around for the kiddies to sit on. Place the tire on the ground and fill the inside of it with sand. Keep it well supplied with spoons, sieves, plastic bottles, cans and toys.

BE A SCRATCH ARTIST

From Colorado: "I have a house full of children, and I get pretty disgusted when their tricycles and toys hit the edge of my furniture. I have **scratches** all over the house, caused by one child or another. Here's how I solved my problem:

"The other day I went to my dime store and bought a box of crayons. I took the black crayon and went over every scratch on my black furniture. With the mahogany furniture I used the dark-brown crayon.

"After this I rubbed and buffed the marks thoroughly with a dry piece of towel.

"The wax from the crayon fills up the scratch and it becomes unnoticeable. I find the crayon much better than iodine."

TEAK TALK

From New Hampshire: "How does one remove the **scratch** from teak wood? Even the furniture store does not know how to keep it looking new or what type of wax to use on it."

After much research, three teak dealers (one an Oriental from the Old Country) tell us that a scratch may be removed by rubbing it gently with 0000 steel wool, then applying *equal* amounts of linseed oil and turpentine. Rub this in well.

We are also informed from all three sources that waxing or polishing is not necessary on genuine teak furniture.

Genuine teak is loaded with its own natural oil. They recommend only polishing it with a cloth that has been dampened with equal parts of turpentine and linseed oil.

SEW BE IT!

A woman from Vermont sent me this letter of interest: "**Sewing** is my hobby and over the years I have learned some shortcuts.

"For years my sewing machine sat in the bedroom and was seldom used because of the trouble and bother of opening it to get ready to sew.

"One day I decided to move all of my sewing equipment to our basement. It has turned out to be the smartest move I ever made. Those who do not have basements could use a laundry room.

"The machine stands open and ready for immediate use at all times. The ironing board stands nearby and a ping-pong table is ideal for a pattern layout. Best of all, I no longer have to put anything away when I stop sewing!

"As as result I find time almost every day to indulge in my hobby. It is amazing the amount of money saved by home sewing. But it isn't only the money—the boost to our ego is wonderful when we find things are done."

From Chicago: "Being a seamstress, I thought I would like to pass on this little hint to others who do their own **sewing.**

"I removed the top drawer of my sewing machine. Turning it over, I drove nails into the bottom of the drawer, pointed side up. I find this most useful for holding all of my spools of thread.

"If people have the new type of machine where the drawer is not removable, they could cut a little piece of plywood to fit the bottom of the drawer and drive the nails through the plywood. Insert the whole kaboodle into the drawer itself. It is most satisfactory."

KEEP SHARP!

From New York: "I keep a piece of sandpaper in my **sewing machine** drawer. This is wonderful to sharpen needles. Just stitch through it a few times and your needle is sharp as new.

"I also keep a blotter in this drawer. Every time I oil my machine, I stitch through the blotter several times. This eliminates the danger of getting oil spots on the material.

"I have a magnet in this drawer, too. This is helpful to pick up dropped pins.

"As a wonderful time and temper saver, I keep a rubber band around all of my spools of thread. I have many different colors. This keeps them from getting tangled, and there is less wasted thread."

WHEN YOU'VE GOT ALL YOUR BUTTONS!

Do you know that if you have a name brand **sewing machine** you can remove the pressure foot (that is the little gadget with the two prongs on it that you feed your material under) and sew on buttons?

You can!

Put your button under the needle, put the needle through one eye, lower the gadget at the back (pressure-foot handle) as if you were doing ordinary sewing, and use your right hand to turn the wheel.

The button, when held with the fingers of your left hand, may be moved back and forth to sew through each eye. Be sure to use your hand for this and not the electrical foot or knee feed.

I found this is the quickest way of sewing buttons on children's clothes, husband's shirt, etc. Try it.

For those who are always losing their **sewing needles:** Push a wad of cotton into the little hole in the spool. Stick the mending needle there. Next time a button comes off, there will be no looking for a needle in that sewing box.

From Maine: "You have no idea how many people do their own **sewing** and have buttonhole attachments. We all use the extra buttons from our button box when making homemade garments.

"When we use our buttonhole attachment, there is no way of telling which attachment will fit the size button we have salvaged to fit the buttonholes we are making. But I have found the solution.

"I took a scrap of material (double thickness) and made samples from each of my templates and made sample button holes, cutting each one open so I could see if a button fit! This way I can take the old button and run it through the 'slit' and see if I have the right plate on my sewing machine.

"I keep the sample cloth in my buttonhole attachment box and when I need to test a button to see if it will go through a hole . . . it's right there.

"I never 'mess' up a garment any more. Nor do I have to go to the store to buy buttons that fit!"

If your husband is always losing shirt buttons, try putting a dab of clear nail polish on the thread in the middle of the button after you **sew** the button back on. I find that this holds the thread.

When **sewing** buttons on a coat or a loosely-woven fabric, we are told that they should not be sewn tightly.

It has always been recommended that the buttons have some sort of object, such as a toothpick or match, held between the eyes of the button and the material before sewing it on so that the button will have enough leeway to keep from ripping the fabric.

Recently I discovered that I could take a fork from my kitchen and hold its tines under the button before sewing it on!

These tines allow just enough space to keep the button from ripping.

SEW AND UN-SEW

For those who **sew** and sometimes make a wrong seam, don't feel bad. Even professional seamstresses do this, and I happen to be one!

There are many ways of ripping seams out and re-doing them, but the easiest way I know is to buy the smallest crochet hook and catch the stitching which must be pulled out with the small hook! It works better than anything I have ever tried. Never snags your material.

And from North Carolina: "In order to remove needle marks from fabrics when you are letting down hems, etc., it is

wise to keep in mind your ultimate purpose . . . to return

the warp and woof threads to the original pattern of the material.

"I use a squeeze bottle with an applicator cap to apply water to the immediate area—if it's safe for that particular material. There is no need to wet the entire garment or the unaffected area. Thoroughly saturate the area to be corrected and let this stand five or ten minutes.

"I place my work on an aluminum fabric-covered ironing board and gently work the damaged area (as in laundering delicate fabrics, remembering the ultimate objective, to return the threads to the original weave). Pulling on the bias gently will usually do the job.

"If not, use the eye end of the needle to work the thread into place. Let the fabric help you by keeping it wet. The fabric must absorb moisture in order to go back into place. Then iron the area dry.

"This works beautifully on hemlines if the crease is brushed first with a stiff brush and then saturated, etc."

Another helpful hint: Keep a small pair of jewelers' pliers in your **sewing basket.** These pliers have long, sharp points and can pick up and pull out the finest and toughest of stitches.

THREAD TRICKS

If the emergency arises for that small **sewing** job and all you have is white thread and need another color . . . try using a crayola (any color you happen to need), and pulling the crayon down the length of the thread once or twice. It will color the white thread.

An item of interest from Denver: "My husband gave me an old roll of nylon fishing line to sew the buttons on my children's clothes. He said at the time he did not believe the kids could pull off the buttons if they were sewn on with this. He was so right. For two years I've not had to sew on buttons and it looks like the fishing line will outlive the coats."

SEAMS EASY!

When stitching heavy seams on your **sewing** machine, rub them with a piece of hard bar soap. The needle will go through the material and won't break.

From Kansas: "I find that when I buy an inexpensive blouse the underarm seam will often rip. Before even wearing blouses I now go to the **sewing** machine and top-stitch the sleeve seam for about three or four inches each side of the side seam. This does not show and it strengthens the seam."

For those who never seem to **sew** sleeves in neatly: Gather the sleeve in place before sewing up the side seam.

This will enable you to work with a flat surface and the little tucks in the gathered section are easily avoided. Then sew the side seams, closing the underside of the sleeve and continuing back on down to the waist.

To keep trouser hems from fraying, **sew** a button one inch from each side of the inside crease and it will relieve friction.

WHEN YOU HAVE A KNOTTY PROBLEM

When **sewing** with a single thread, does it constantly knot? If so, try this: After you thread the needle, be sure to knot the end that was cut off closest to the spool. Thread is woven this way!

WHEN IT'S PORTABLE

From Georgia: "Surely lots of busy housewives have portable **sewing machines.** When I sew I put mine on my adjustable ironing board! I always get just the right height."

From Ohio: "Since I keep my portable **sewing machine** up most of the time, I made a terry cloth cover for it . . . using the cover on my toaster as a pattern. It looks real pretty and keeps my sewing machine free of dust. Also it saves me from getting it out and putting it away each time I have something to mend."

If you glue a piece of foam rubber to the bottom of a portable **sewing machine** foot control, it won't creep on the floor!

A word of caution from Oregon: "Advise the girls to keep their **sewing machines** oiled. Mine just stopped recently! The repairman came, applied some oil, and it works fine now.

Could save others a service call. Directions are in the booklet that comes with your machine."

MACHINE MAID

A paper bag taped to the **sewing machine** makes it easier to keep threads and bits of material from littering the floor. Much easier than trying to "hit" the wastebasket.

From a dry cleaner: "When you're **sewing** long pieces of material such as draperies, etc., it is better to clip the selvage at four-inch intervals if it must be left on. The seam will not pucker when dry cleaned if selvages are clipped."

From Honolulu: "I finally found a way to patch those narrow-legged blue jeans my boys wear for play. My neighbor showed me. She merely rips the outside seam (not the inner, flatfelled one) for about ten inches along the knee area. She then flattens out the leg and **sews** the patch on. Then she re-stitches the seam. This is much easier than struggling the way I have been doing."

From Maine: "Can you think of anything more frustrating than trying to **sew** scout or military emblems on a uniform so they are straight?

"I've got the solution:

"Just use a few dabs of any good white household glue on the back of the emblem and press it in position on the clothing, then let it set for a few moments.

"The emblem can then be stitched by hand or machine without any worry that it will turn out lop-sided. The glue subsequently washes out, too."

SNAPPY TALK

When applying **snaps** to any garment, sew all of the small portions of the snap (with the little point) on the garment first. Then take a piece of chalk and touch this little point. Turn your material over, rub it with your finger . . . and you will find that you will have marked the exact place where the snap should be sewed on the other side! Just sew the other portion of the snap on the chalked dot.

GROWING ROOM

From Kentucky: "When I make my daughter's little dresses, I always take an extra one-inch tuck on the inside of the hem.

"I run the 'tuck' up on the **sewing machine** with a big basting stitch. I do this on any part of the inside of the hem, although I find it better to do it near the bottom of the dress.

"When the child grows another inch or two and the hem needs lengthening, just remove the basting stitch that holds the tuck and the dress will drop two inches. No hem to replace either."

CINDERELLA STORY!

I have made a wonderful discovery which I know will interest all of you who have dyed-to-match satin shoes.

Recently a friend ruined two pairs of satin shoes. One pair was red and the other was blue.

The two pairs of shoes were water-spotted. The woman was caught in the rain in one pair, and she walked across damp grass in the other. She had taken them to two shoe shops and they told her that the shoes could be redyed, but they would not guarantee removing or covering the spots.

We sent one pair out to another shoe shop. Almost the same answer came back: "We can redye these shoes but they must be a darker color [which would not match the dress at all] and we won't guarantee them."

I worried about these for two weeks.

One day the dawn brought daylight. If moisture caused the spots, why wouldn't moisture take them out? Water refused to work . . . *never use water* on this type of shoe.

So, I tried experimenting again. I went back to my old favorite item: *vinegar!*

I dipped a terry cloth washrag in distilled white vinegar (and I don't know why some other types wouldn't do), wrung it out *well*, and started wiping with the grain of the satin. Immediately, all the water spots came out!

Just to compare, I cleaned only one shoe of each color and let them dry overnight by *natural* air. It was a complete success.

Now, here come the secrets I learned:

Don't try to quick-dry the shoes by putting them in a window or the sunshine. Leave them in the shade and let them dry slowly and naturally.

Gals, some of this dye will come off on your hands, but it can be removed with a weak solution of bleach (I'm not allergic), or you could wear rubber gloves.

Satin shoes may often be redyed at the store where they were purchased. Ask your salesman if this service is available when buying your shoes.

Keep your satin shoes in plastic bags. This will keep them from absorbing "vapors" from the air and humidity.

Never try to spot-clean satin shoes. It will leave another ring. The entire shoe must be cleaned at the same time even though the rest of the shoe is not dirty.

Never rub against the grain of the satin. Ruins it.

Don't get your washrag too wet with vinegar. Be sure to wring it out well before applying it to the satin. This is most important.

Ladies, if you want to take a chance and clean your own shoes, try this vinegar method.

We tried it on red, blue, pink and pale green dyed satin shoes. Then we tried it on black satin. It's fantastic! When you're doing black satin, I suggest that you take a soft brush or cloth and dust them well first, with the grain of the satin, to remove all the dust before applying the vinegar rub. No point in imbedding the dust and dirt and trying to make mud pies!

THE SHOE MUST GO ON!

Do you have a pair of **shoes** with a worn inner sole? And hate to spend money to have it replaced? Here's my answer: Remove the old worn inner sole from your shoe and place it on top of some adhesive-backed plastic and cut a new one! Any scrap of it you happen to have around the house will do. Remove thin film from back and stick the new innersole in shoe.

If you buy some, I suggest you purchase black. It sure looks neat in my shoes!

Those summer white **shoes** get dirty so fast, especially when you are on your way to an appointment and want to look your best!

Carry a piece of white chalk in your purse and use it for a quick touch-up. It does wonders, especially on cloth or suede shoes.

DRY RUN

From California: "For mothers with children who wear tennis **shoes** and often need them in a hurry:

"Wash them and use a towel to dry as much as possible. Then get your hair dryer out and turn it on 'high.' Put the hair dryer into the shoe itself and after about eight minutes (for each shoe) they are ready to wear!

"No more waiting for them to drip dry, especially when you are in a hurry and need them quickly."

From Minneapolis: "I have found that I can save time and **shoe leather** with white and light-colored smooth-leather shoes by putting a coat of clear shoe polish on them the minute they come home from the store.

"I don't even polish shoes after this and only renew the application once or twice a season.

"Dirt simply wipes off, if, indeed, any sticks. This also prevents spotting from liquids dropped or splashed on the shoes."

Others say that a thin coat of colorless paste floor wax also will do the trick.

If you have an old pair of canvas or linen **shoes** which *were* white, they can be easily tinted for a few more wearings.

Get a tube of white shoe cleaner, squeeze some into an old saucer and add food coloring. Then mix this well.

Apply as you would white shoe polish and presto . . . pink, yellow, blue or even green shoes. Start by using pale colors. The next time you can change the color or go to darker shades.

From Pennsylvania: "I have found an attractive way to patch those girls' and boys' worn-out tennis **shoes.**

"Where the holes are . . . try sewing on a button! Or embroider a buttonhole with a colored thread, and then apply the button.

"Also, it has become a fad in my town to sew patches of different shapes out of heavy material to cover the holes. This looks really good."

SUCCESS ON A SHOESTRING!

From Boston: "I've got five kids and they all wear tennis **shoes!** I got so sick of washing the shoelaces that I finally set up a system.

"My system was to buy two pairs of extra tennis shoelaces and *keep* a jar—I use an old fruit jar—with water and a bleach solution in it with the lid on tight. I find that if you do not tightly cap a jar containing bleach solution, it tends to lose its strength.

"Place the shoelaces in the jar and let them soak a day or so. They come clean every time. The next time you wash a pair of tennis shoes, you will have a bleached, clean pair of laces without waiting for them to dry."

When the plastic ends come off children's **shoelaces**, thread them through the holes again and tie a knot so the frayed ends cannot slip back out through the holes. Saves rethreading next day, etc.

SHINING HOURS

From Illinois: "I clean my baby's white **shoes** with rubbing alcohol! After cleaning the smudges off with the alcohol, I let them dry and then polish the shoes."

Just try shining your husband's **shoes** with an old nylon stocking instead of a rag. They shine like glass.

From Wisconsin: "I save my husband's worn socks and use them to pull over a shoe brush when I'm buffing our **shoes!** Keeps the brush clean.

"By using a different sock for each color of shoes that I polish, I never have to worry about one color of polish coming off on another color shoe.

"Children's socks make ideal applicators for paste polish."

From New York: "I use powder puffs to polish my **shoes** and find they do a perfect job.

"I buy a different powder puff for each color shoe. When they're not in use, I keep the puffs in the plastic bags they came in so the different colored polishes won't rub against one another."

From Michigan: "Don't throw away that old bread box . . . it makes the handiest **shoeshine box** imaginable! Especially for the children and Dad.

"I gave mine a fast coat of black paint, inside and out.

When it dried, I put some colorful decals on it. It can hold everything that's needed to polish the shoes. And the top is plenty roomy to put your foot on for the shine job, so that the polish never touches the floor!"

From Virginia: "After your broom has been worn down to stubble, don't throw it away.

"Have your husband cut off the handle about halfway, then dig a small hole in the ground near your back door and push the broom handle into the ground. Fill the hole around the metal part of the broom so that just the stubble sticks out. You have the best **shoe-scraper** ever . . . and for free!"

A SHOWER OF IDEAS

A young bachelor from Washington writes: "Just how would you keep a **shower** curtain from flapping over the edge of the shower? Every time I take a shower, my bathroom floor is a mess of water!"

My answer is that I would look for a fishing equipment store and buy some fish line weights!

Now, since you cannot sew, stop at a dime store and buy a small package of safety pins. Run the safety pins through the fish line weights and attach them along the bottom of the shower curtain.

These weights will keep the shower curtain from flapping. It is the water pressure which sends the shower curtain flying!

Let me share my find with those of you who have mildew on the bottom of your shower curtain.

Just take your pinking shears and cut off that ol' hem. This way, the water cannot accumulate on the bottom of your **shower curtain** and mildew cannot possibly absorb and "grow" across the bottom of it. I find that the water hits the shower curtain, runs completely down the length of the curtain and has no place to stop!

With the pinking finish across the bottom, the water will hit these little zig-zags and drop right back into the shower!

Wax **shower** curtain hooks and rods with paste wax. The hooks will slide easily and the wax will help keep the rod from rusting.

From Indianapolis: "I would like to tell you what I did to an unsightly glass **shower door.** I first cleaned it with a soap pad and rinsed it well with vinegar and then clear water.

"When the door was dry, I painted the inside of it with fish aquarium paint. I found this in the pet department of the dime store. It comes in colors and costs about twenty-five cents a bottle. It took only two bottles to paint one door.

"This gave my door a frosted appearance, like the frost on a windowpane. If you are imaginative, fancy designs can be made, too."

TAPE TIPS HIM OFF!

From Kentucky: "To help my husband choose a **shirt** at a glance, I iron on a piece of colored tape over the label at the back of the neck of those older shirts that are frayed at the collars and cuffs or are patched. A small piece of tape will do.

"This way, he just has to look at the label in the back of the collar without unfolding the entire shirt.

"If he needs a perfect shirt, he looks for one without the colored tape over the label. If he is going someplace that doesn't demand perfection, he looks for a shirt with a colored 'wife label' in the back of the collar. Saves lots of time and messy drawers and closet shelves."

A SHORT STORY

Some of us who are not "short-shorts" lovers would like to be able to find a pair that fits us and is cut exactly at the right length. For instance, some of us would wear **shorts** if we could find them cut just below the knees.

Watch for slacks and peddlepushers on *sale*. When you find a pair that fits, *buy it*.

While you are in the store, look for a white blouse. Often there are blouses on sale at the same time.

When you go home, cut the slacks or peddlepushers off to the exact length you desire, leaving about an inch and a half for a good hem. These may be either hemmed by hand or on the sewing machine. And don't throw the leg part away. We are going to use that to make a darling outfit!

Slit open the sides of the part you cut off (where the inseam is) and spread out. Lay the collar of the white shirt that you just bought on this piece of material. Cut exactly around the collar and make your pattern for a new colored collar! Use your iron and turn this new colored collar under one-fourth of an inch all the way around.

Cover the original shirt collar with the extra piece of material you have left from these peddlepushers. Not only does it make a snazzy outfit, but that printed collar won't show soil as much as a white one does!

This matching collar may be stitched on top of the original white one with a sewing machine or appliquéd, or even sewn by hand with a blind stitch.

With the leftover scraps you can make a binding for the top of one pocket or, if the shirt does not have pockets (and I absolutely despise shirts that do not have *two* pockets), you can make two pockets to match the collar and the shorts.

Another cute idea is to cut out little squares or triangles of this extra material (about an inch square or so) and sew them on the blouse so that it will look like a patched checkerboard. On one set, I saw these little squares and triangles sewn just on the white pockets and the collar itself. Really makes for a darling outfit which costs you practically nothing if you *watch* for your *sales!*

MANY A SLIP . . .

From Maine: "All women wear **slips.** But sometimes the tops wear out first. There is no need to discard the slip. I cut the worn part off and make a hem at the waistline, then thread elastic through and have a new half-slip.

"Whole slips are beautiful but usually expensive, so this is quite a saving in my budget.

"Also, those who have older slips, which are longer than today's styles, can cut them in half and make two garments out of one!

"Naturally, as short as today's dresses are, the waistline can be cut lower down on the garment. Save that upper half to wear with thin blouses and under sweaters. Just use your *pinking shears* to cut the waist, and no hemming is necessary —it will not ravel.

"By making your own camisole from an old slip and cutting it with pinking shears, you will have no tell-tale line that will show through your skirts or slacks. And they can be tinted different colors with packaged dyes. You needn't use an entire package of dye for these small garments. A small portion will suffice.

"I got this brainstorm from the old slips when I cleaned out my dresser drawer and found six slips that I was saving for the day when dresses would get longer.

"It dawned on me—why should I wait—dresses seem to be getting shorter and shorter. I couldn't bear to throw these slips away, so I cut them in two and now I not only have emptier dresser drawers, but new slips, too.

"These camisoles are great for working girls who wear skirts that are already lined. There is no need to wear two slips: just wear the upper half!"

From Cleveland: "This is my answer to women who complain about nylon **slips** clinging to their bodies. I have prevented this for years by using dusting powder (bath powder, etc.) inside my slips. I also use powder on the inside of my husband's trousers, which were clinging to his legs. Powder even stops jersey dresses from clinging to my body."

IN SHORT . . .

From New York: "To shorten my **slips** which are too long . . . I sew a tuck on the outside of the slip just above the trim at the hem.

"Too, when longer dresses do come back into style all one has to do is rip out this little row of stitching and the slip will be lengthened again."

HERE'S NEWS ON SLIPCOVERS

If your **slipcovers** slip, try this:

Crush a newspaper up and stick it down in the back (underneath the cushion) and the sides. This will prevent the arms from sagging and the front of the cover from slipping. If one newspaper isn't enough, use two or three. Chairs vary in size and some covers are looser than others.

Pins can be bought and used for this purpose but often, when you remove your slipcovers for cleaning, you will find a torn place where the pin was.

Sometimes when you remove your slipcovers, even on brand new furniture, you will find a dirty spot on the arms and pillow back. Why? Because you have let your covers get too soiled and the soil has worked itself through the material and soaked into your upholstery.

There are two main places where this will happen—arms and headrest sections. This can be prevented by covering the chair arms and pillow back with plastic before putting the slipcovers on! Plastic bags that clothes come in are good for this.

The spot is caused by the natural oils from our bodies. There is no way (that I know of) to prevent this. Oil from the hair causes the pillow to soil.

Slipcovers must be kept clean. This also prolongs the life of your covers.

If you are contemplating new slipcovers, think about buying lightweight upholstery material. At least look at it first.

This material doesn't cost much more than regular slipcover material. Sometimes it is cheaper if you can get it on sale. It has other good points, too. It doesn't look so much like a slipcover and will give you better protection for your furniture if you spill something. Upholstery material can be dry cleaned and does not soil as easily as a thin material that is wet cleaned.

Some slipcovers are filled with dust. If you doubt this, look at your coffee table and see how much dust it accumulates in a week. Think how many weeks' dust is in your covers!

Dust in slipcovers and all cloth, for that matter, causes rotting. Remove the dust by putting your slipcovers in your drier. Let them tumble about twenty minutes without heat. Replace and they will look grand!

If water is spilled (or perspiration soaks) on dusty cloth, it will cause "ring spots." If there is no dust you will not get a brown "dust ring," which is almost impossible to remove.

Here's an idea from Florida: "I always place a piece of aluminum foil on the arms of my sofa and chairs before putting on my **slipcovers.** This prevents the soil from penetrating through the slipcovers into the upholstery."

From Texas: "I take **slipcovers** out of the drier slightly damp, put them on the furniture, and smooth them with my hands. They look as if they have been pressed."

From Idaho: "When buying material for **slipcovers** (or having them made), I always get an extra yard or two. Each time the covers are dry cleaned or washed, include this extra piece of material with the covers themselves.

"The arms of the chairs always wear out first. When this happens, the worn piece of material may be carefully ripped from the slipcover and used for a perfect pattern! Then just place the new piece where the old one originally was.

"Stitch this on the machine, or by hand if you are a good seamstress and have no machine.

"I find that I can get another two or three years of wear from my slipcovers by doing this."

WAX YOUR SKILLET

Sent by a confirmed bachelor: "When you get through washing your cast-iron **skillet,** take a piece of wax paper, and while the skillet is still warm, wipe around the inside. This will prevent rusting.

"Be sure the skillet is not too hot. All you want is a little bit of wax to fill the pores of the cast iron. And don't burn your hands! Be sure to use enough waxed paper."

STEAK MAGIC

The next time you have **steak**, try marinating it briefly in French dressing . . . then broil as usual. Delicious!

SALAD TARGET: ALL OVER

Tip from kitchen lover: "I use a great deal of oil and vinegar in **salads** and for cooking. So I have learned to keep a pair of matched spray bottles on my counter top, one filled with vinegar and the other with oil.

"They not only look better than the ordinary oil and vinegar bottles, but I can just squirt the oil and vinegar over my lettuce. This gives a better range than just dumping them on all in one spot."

SWEET TRICK

From Kentucky: "I have found that I can make my own super-fine **sugar** in an emergency by using my blender."

IT'S ALL IN THE BLEND!

Did you know that when you make barbecue **sauce**, which usually calls for chopped lemons, onions, etc., you could put them in your blender, let it run for a few minutes and that it would actually be a purée. Then cook.

Instead of making it for one meal at a time, double it, pour the excess in a jar and freeze it.

SOAP'S ON!

From Montana: "I wax my bars of **soap** on one side so they always serve as their own soap dishes. I can use the soap right down to the last dab this way and there never is any waste.

"I melt a small amount of paraffin about a half- to a quarter-inch deep and place all my bars of soap in it for just a second. Remove the bars of soap from the paraffin and turn them upside down to cool. This prevents the paraffin from sticking to anything.

"The thin sheet of wax allows the bar of soap to be put anywhere and it will not melt, get mushy or adhere to a wash basin or soap dish."

From Maryland: "Our answer to slippery shower **soap** is to drop the bar of soap into the toe of a nylon hose, tie a knot to form a wrist loop in the top of the stocking, and enjoy the bonus of a gentle scrubbing action from the nylon! A different color of soap for each family member is a suggestion."

From Georgia: "I buy a large sponge and cut it up into small sponges so they will fit in the exact space in the **soap** tray, which is recessed in the wall by my bathtub. I then put the soap on the sponge.

"When finished with our bath, we use this sponge to clean the tub. It is full of soap and does an excellent cleaning job.

"I cut the same type of sponge into smaller pieces and put them under the soap on the sink, too. This leaves no soap residue to clean up afterward. There is also no need for a special cloth for cleaning the bathroom fixtures."

From New Hampshire: "A satisfactory way to utilize those bits of **soap** that are left is to make a slash (the length of the soap) in the side of a sponge, not cutting it *all* the way through. The sponge will look like an envelope. Insert the soap pieces in the pocket, and when the sponge is dampened, it's handy for many purposes!"

SPRINGING BACK TO LIFE

Do you have a chair or sofa suffering from sagging **springs**?

Turn the piece of furniture upside down. Make a paper pattern of the under-structure frame. Go to any lumber yard and buy a piece of scrap masonite and nail this to the underside of the chair.

In olden times people used to put what we call a templet on the bottoms of their chairs. But nowadays, springs which are sagging and those which have broken webbing can usually be given a new lease on life by the simple method of buying masonite, or even one-eighth-inch plywood. Just nail it on the bottom of the furniture. Now let me tell you what this does:

Ordinarily, people pay to have springs retied and the bottoms of chairs rewebbed. By nailing a piece of plywood or masonite onto the bottom of the chair, the springs are pushed back up into the chair and you can easily get at least five more years of wear out of that piece of furniture.

And the springs will behave properly! This idea is for people who want to "make do" with furniture which otherwise would be done over—or done in.

TAMING OF THE SCREW

Here's a very good hint for those who have wood **screws** that keep coming out of furniture.

Try putting a piece of steel wool in the hole itself and then threading the screw back in! You'll be surprised at the result.

WHEN YOU FEEL YOURSELF SLIPPING . . .

From Florida: "We bought a sectional **sofa** with square legs and then found that the sections separated at odd moments—as when an unwary guest sat on the crack between the sections!

"Rubber caps did not fit under the square legs. Then my husband's mother suggested small squares of foam rubber the size of the legs themselves. Result? No more slips, 'wiggles' and separations, and best of all the foam rubber doesn't even show."

A woman from Oregon wanted to know how to keep furniture in place when it was not directly against the wall: "Every time we sit on our **sofa,** it slides against the wall and makes a mark," she wrote.

I presume she does not have carpets. In that case, I told her to go to a dime store and buy some rubber "castor cups" and place them under each leg of her sofa. I specifically suggest the rubber types as they seem to hold much better on bare floors than glass castors and are very inexpensive.

From Washington: "My **sofa** was always being pushed against the wall and was making a mark, so I screwed a few doorstops with rubber tips into the wooden frame at the back of the couch! Now my walls are protected."

AN OIL-FASHIONED REMEDY

From a reader: "To remove fresh grease or oil **stains** from clothing: place the garment over a flat surface such as an ironing board and sprinkle talcum powder over the spot. Work this in well with your fingers and let set awhile; then brush out with a stiff brush. Do this *before* laundering.

"One application will usually remove the oil or grease. I have never found this method to spot or to leave a circle."

WHEN YOU'VE GOT YOUR HANDS FULL

For removing **stains** on fingers: Lemon juice is wonderful. Squeeze the juice of a lemon into a very small container and soak your fingers in it. And something extra: the juice makes it easy to push the cuticle! Afterward, gently brush your fingers with mild hand soap and warm water and rinse well. Use your favorite hand cream . . . and just see the difference!

From Virginia: "When I get fruit and gardening **stains** on my hands, I use peroxide and liquid soap. It gets the stains from the fine lines in my hands and around my fingernails. I then rinse in cold water and use hand cream."

SPOT THOSE STAINS

From Philadelphia: "I happen to be the owner of seven cleaning establishments. I would like some help from you and I feel sure that all of my competitors would, too.

"Women, God bless them, are wonderful. We wouldn't have any business if it weren't for them. But they could do the grandest thing not only for us but also for themselves if they would remember to do one thing: When they have a **stain** on a garment—whether it be clothing or blankets—it would eliminate many problems if they would take a piece of scratch paper and write down what the stain is and then take a safety pin and pin the paper to the very spot itself.

"Our spotters cannot help but see a safety pin. They can then read the note and know exactly what to do to remove that special spot. Example: 'Coffee stain, with cream and sugar.' We use entirely different methods of cleaning for coffee stains that do not contain cream or sugar.

"Sometimes spotters will not see a damaged area. Therefore we send the article through the regular cycle. Then steam pressing sets many stains, and it's too late!"

COLOR ME DESPERATE

From Illinois: "My child left crayons in the pocket of his blue jeans. I didn't discover them until after the jeans had been through the drier! What can I do?"

I have had so many letters like this that I wrote to an excellent home economist for advice. Here is her answer:

"On the crayon **stain** question, which is a fairly common one . . . we sometimes despair. However, there are certain things that can be done. As you undoubtedly know, crayons are much like lipstick. They contain grease, wax and dye.

"The grease and wax can be easily removed by cleaning the clothes in any good dry cleaning solvent, but sometimes the dye remains. This dye may be taken out if the clothes are cleaned with a dry cleaning fluid immediately and, of course, a good nonflammable solvent will remove the stains from the drier.

"Another suggestion—sometimes a safe, all-purpose, all-fabric sodium perborate bleach (this is powdered and is sold under various names) will help. For persistent stains, such as this dye from the crayons, I make a sort of paste of the powdered perborate bleach (be sure it is *not* a *chlorine* bleach) and put this on the moistened fabric where the stain is. Keep it moist and give it time. Often the dye comes out.

"As a last resort, your professional cleaner has spotting agents for removal of dye, but I don't trust myself to use these. I think a professional is needed to spot clean."

SCOUR THAT SCORCH!

From Montana: "I **scorched** a white cotton blouse and tried everything to remove it, to no avail. Finally I decided to use a household scouring cleanser that contained bleach. After wetting the material, I poured some cleanser on and took a handbrush and rubbed it on my blouse. It took it out beautifully!

"I do not know if this would work on any other kind of material but it certainly works on cotton."

Ladies, I have tried this and it does work! It seems that the household cleansers that contain bleach have just enough to remove some types of scorching. Be sure to wet the material thoroughly first and test the spot before using this method.

However, I have never yet found it to ruin any white cotton material.

From Ohio: "This may seem like a joke, but I rub my **scorches** with a piece of raw onion and leave them for a short time. I then soak them in cold water . . . the marks fade!"

KEEP DIRT OUT WITH STARCH

From Georgia: "My husband wears starched uniforms to work. I have to wash and iron six each week. Please tell me what I can do about the mud, rain and soil stains on the legs of his trousers. As he gets in and out of his truck when it rains, these **stains** sometimes go as high as the knee."

Try using plain *boiled* starch.

After taking the garment from the washing machine and while the garment is still thoroughly wet, dip the pants into warm, boiled starch up to the knee (you can go further if you want to), then proceed as usual.

When these mud and dirt stains get on the trousers thereafter they will stick to the starch and not work themselves into the fibers of the fabric.

When you wash the starch out next time you wash the trousers, the dirt will also leave!

THIS WON'T TAKE THE STARCH OUT OF YOU

If you have a big load of **starching,** use the washing machine method. Cook your starch (cold water starch is O.K., too), and *after* your machine has completed its cycle and spun dry, pour the starch solution in your washing machine. Let the load agitate for a while again. Then just spin it dry!

If there are not lots of starched things or other items to be dampened, I have found it best to remove the clothes from the line that are ready to be put away, and leave everything on the line which will need sprinkling.

Here's why: It's easier!

You can sprinkle the clothes while they are still on the line. Use your garden hose. Just turn the nozzle to fine spray and sprinkle away.

Gals, it's fantastic. Stand back a little way from the clothes and let that fine spray do all the work for you. You can sprinkle twenty times as fast! More evenly, too. Saves getting clothes too wet or having spots which aren't wet enough.

Then put these clothes away in your plastic bag to sit overnight . . . they will be well "oiled" and ready for a quick ironing the next morning.

Besides, you are *not* (I hope) going to iron the same day you do five loads of laundry. Take a rest with the time you have saved by using this method.

For those of you who have only light starching, try this: *After* you have sprinkled your clothes lightly with the fine spray on your garden hose, remove those which need to be sprinkled only with water, put them in the bag and set aside. Then take your spray bottle of starch (whether you make your own or buy it ready-prepared makes no difference), and while the clothes are still hanging (you have already removed all the others), go back with that bottle of starch and work that plunger up and down with your finger . . .

Spray starch everything in sight. If something needs a little heavier starching, such as a shirt collar, give it a second squirt before taking the clothes down. It's quick, easy, and energy-saving!

Here's another good reason for starching on the line:

You have already sprayed your garments with water. The water will moisten the fibers on the fabric and the starch takes a far better "hold."

How did I figure this out? Because most clothes should be starched while they are still wet, or else rewetted. Perhaps you are not in the mood to starch *then* . . . you have more loads of laundry to do, children yelling, phone ringing and you are tired. So just let those clothes dry and then rewet them with the hose, and starch while still on the line.

So something needs real heavy starching? Restarch it later on your ironing board with more of that goop in your spray bottle. It's the only answer to quick starching.

Always put these starched things in a plastic bag after they are sprinkled and starched. Leave *overnight*. Far easier to iron! Those of you who don't get around to doing the ironing next day, put the plastic bag chock full of clothes in your refrig. They'll keep days without mildew. If you are really pressed for time and iron when you get around to it . . . try your deep freeze! Clothes may be left in the deep freeze, starched or not. They will not mildew, and they will stay for weeks, just waiting for you.

So happy ironing while your clothes are cold! They iron so much easier, quicker and nicer. Try it. Doesn't cost you a copper penny.

STARCH TO THE RESCUE

From Nevada: "I had trouble pressing the edges of a piece of bias facing so that I could baste it in place. In desperation, I *sprayed* the bias tape with good old spray **starch** and presto, like magic, it stayed down. Not only that, but when I found one side wasn't what I wanted, I sprayed it again and erased the first pressing. I used this trick on cotton and taffeta also and it works!"

If your nylon dress hems roll up, try ironing them on the wrong side. Lightly spray the inside of the hem with **starch** before pressing.

From South Carolina: "Here's what I do to prevent perspiration stains from leaving ugly rings around the armholes of my cotton dresses and blouses. Before they are even worn for the first time, I turn the garments inside out, spray the underarms with spray **starch** (not plastic) and then iron dry. Then I repeat this on the right side of the material.

"When I iron a dress or blouse completely, I spray the outer side of the armhole extra heavily with starch. I repeat this procedure each time the garment is washed and ironed. I have done this for several months and all perspiration stains just float away when I wash my cotton dresses or blouses.

"Some people prefer cooked starch for everyday use, but a

can of spray starch would be a wise investment used right over other starches.

"I also give my daughter's play clothes an extra heavy spray on the seat of her shorts and slacks, and the dirt rolls away when they're washed."

It is a fact that starch, when applied to certain fabrics, puts a coat over the fibers. I find that a thin spray of starch (not the plastic type) does help prevent perspiration rings and soil marks from becoming imbedded in the fibers of many materials, especially cottons. Why not apply a thin coat of starch to absorb these stains so they may be easily washed out, rather than let them soak into the fibers where they are hard to loosen? As the starch washes out each washday, the stains and bacteria will be easier to remove. I *still* highly recommend using a vinegar rinse (one-fourth cup to each two quarts of water) to rinse *anything* washable that has bacteria or perspiration odors.

From Kentucky: "I do not have much **storage space,** so I store my extra blankets between my mattresses and bedsprings."

SWEETER SWEATERS

From Utah: "You may think I am crazy, but I use shampoo to launder my **sweaters.** I find that the results are soft and clean-smelling sweaters.

"And something else, too: A sweater will not stretch when you rinse it in a colander and gently squeeze out the excess water."

From Minneapolis: "After you wash **sweaters,** fold them in half and lay them on top of your washer or drier or some porcelain household appliance to dry.

"When dry, they are beautifully pressed. I always put my heavier sweaters on top of the drier, and they benefit because of the warmth, which hastens the drying process."

SWEATER, GIRL?

From California: "Did you know that if you wear a size thirty-four blouse, a size thirty-eight **sweater** will look much better on you? Not only does the sweater not pull, but the sleeve is cut deeper.

"Too, I find that when some sweaters are washed, they do not always go back to their original size. Therefore, I now buy sweaters two sizes larger than my blouse size, and when the sweaters are washed, they fit perfectly, even without ironing!"

t

TABLE TALK

Do you use a lace **tablecloth** on your dining-room table every day? And do the children spill salt and sugar? During the week, don't remove the cloth and everything that stays on the table. Just remove the brush on the end of your vacuum and let the tube suck up those spills!

From New Jersey: "We have a round dining-room table. Finding the proper **table mats** to use on it was a problem until I thought of plastic (the kind used for upholstering).

"I bought one-half yard of plastic and, using my pinking shears, cut it into four even pieces, twelve by eighteen inches.

"I set each piece of plastic on the table and cut one edge of it to fit the curve of the table itself! We have used these mats every day for years and they are as good as new."

From Ohio: "I heard of your suggestion to put a dab of mayonnaise on dining room **table tops** to remove scratches and so forth.

"Well . . . I bought a whole pint! I slopped it all over the top of the table and left it for a while. Then I removed it and rubbed hard with soft, old rags.

"My twenty-year-old table was so pretty that I used the mayonnaise treatment on all my coffee tables!"

ROLL 'EM!

From Old-Fashioned: "To those gals who still use such **table settings** as doilies, place mats and fancy fingertip linen towels—no need to spend hours ironing, only to have them crushed in the linen cabinet. After they are ironed, I roll mine on the cardboard tube which comes inside of a roll of paper towels.

"This eliminates creases from folding, takes up less space in your cabinet and saves repressing."

WAFFLE YOUR TOAST

From Florida: "Have you ever tried making **toast** in your waffle iron? Butter both sides and cook as you would a waffle. Beautiful checkered toast."

T-SHIRT TIP

From Alaska: "When washing men's and boys' **T-shirts,** I stretch them in length while they are still wet, before I hang them on the line. I have found that they stretch considerably and retain their correct length.

"I never hang T-shirts by the edge. I fold them over the line four or five inches from the bottom, then pin with the clothespins. You will find that they keep their shape much better."

A BETTER-LOOKING SEAT

I am flooded with letters wanting to know how to paint a **toilet seat.** I have tried painting with a brush. This was the biggest mess. Never use a brush! Takes too long to dry and leaves brush marks. Besides, knowing the average housewife, she will go to the garage and see what kind of "left-over" white paint she has and just slop some on.

Take it from me, gals, just *any* kind of paint cannot be used to paint toilet seats! Cheap paint turns yellow. Brushes leave marks and the toilet seat looks worse than it did before it was ever painted. Mine did. I had to buy a new one, and I couldn't even wait for a sale. I paid full price! That's how bad it was.

Then I tried spray paints. Buy the best spray paint you can afford when you want to paint the toilet seat. Don't try to save pennies here.

I found the best paint came in a small can. (Don't buy a pint can—it's quite unnecessary. Buy the smallest you can find. Go to a store where they sell model airplanes and hot rod equipment. They have cans of paint in tiny sizes at half, and less, the price of big cans.)

There are low-pressure, "fizz" cans of paint that are great for the toilet seat.

First, wait until your family leaves the house for the day. Unscrew the toilet seat. This may take a special Phillips head screwdriver. If you don't have one, try using a paring knife or a tiny screwdriver.

Then wash the toilet seat. I rinsed mine with a vinegar water solution and dried it with a bath towel.

Take the toilet seat *outside* (sprays from "fizz" cans can damage carpets, walls and surrounding objects), and place it on newspapers on the grass or garage floor.

Spray the bottom of the seat first. Then the back of the lid. Let this dry. Really, this needs only one coat. Then, turn the seat and the lid over and spray.

I have found that this job should not be done in the direct sun. The seat gets too hot and the paint dries too fast. Better to do it in the shade.

Or paint it in the morning and then let it dry in the sun while the day is still cool.

Now, ladies, I have the prettiest toilet seat in town! It's shiny, clean, and cost less than a dollar! And I still have paint left. Good paint. Surprising how far good paint goes. What is left over can be used for many things.

And gals, while you are at this job, remove the chrome

fittings (if they will come loose) and clean them with turpentine. If you don't have turpentine, use kerosene. It's just as good for this purpose.

"Fizz" paint comes in colors. You don't have to buy white. If you're color-minded, look at the chart before you buy.

One more thing about "fizz" paint cans . . . after you are through painting, turn the can upside down and press the spray button a few seconds. This will clear out the excess paint in the nozzle so that you can use the left-over paint later. If this is not done, the can will get stopped up. Sure, you will waste a little paint when you do this, but think of the paint you will save in the long run!

KEEPING THE LID ON

From North Carolina: "Every time I buy a **toilet lid cover,** the piece of twine which ties it on either end gets broken or lost in the hem. What can I do with the covers, besides discarding them?"

You can go to a dime store and buy an *extra long* shoelace. Cut the tip of the shoelace off on one end and stick a safety pin through it. You can then use it as a threader to run back through the little hem itself. This will have to be done about two inches at a time, depending on the size of your safety pin.

However, here's what I did to mine: Instead of using bias tape or shoelaces, I used narrow elastic. After running the elastic through the hem I just tied a knot in it and presto! I don't have any more strings to hang, knots to tie or broken threads. Also, the elastic helps hold the cover in place.

For those who like to have their bath towels match their toilet lid covers, use a bath towel and make your own cover.

Allow about two inches extra all around the edge, turn under and stitch a hem. Then thread it through with string or narrow elastic.

SQUEEZE PLAY

For that last dab of **toothpaste** in the (usually bent) tube: Just hold the tube under the hot water faucet and squeeze . . . every last bit of paste will come out easily!

TOYING WITH A FEW IDEAS

Here are a few hints on cleaning children's **toys.**

From Maryland: "We use cornstarch to clean fuzzy stuffed animals. We just rub the cornstarch on the fuzzy part and let it stand a few minutes. Then we brush out the cornstarch and the toys are clean once more. We use the cornstarch as it comes out of the box . . . dry."

From Rhode Island: "I use mild soap and warm water to wash stuffed **toys,** woolly or otherwise. Toss them into your automatic washer and drier and that's all there is to it, if the stuffing permits.

"But do not place toys with plastic faces in your drier. They come out like well-masticated bubblegum! Hang them in the sun or a warm area in your home. Give a slight brushing after they are dry. That's all there is to it!"

From Virginia: "I use commercial-type furniture upholstery cleaners to clean my children's stuffed **toys.** I clean them just as one would an ordinary chair, and then hang the animals on the line to dry. It even made the matted hair on the toys stand up!"

TRIP TIPS

From Missouri: "When you're taking a **trip** in a car with youngsters who play in the back of the car and fall asleep . . . always take along a few pillows.

"These are wonderful when Father is driving and Mother (or one of the kiddies) wants to nap. Saves lots of backaches, too. You can pile up a few bed pillows and the youngsters sleep peacefully on them.

"I have found it best to take a favorite bed pillow and put three pillowslips on it, one over the other. When the top slip gets soiled, slip it off and fold it in your suitcase. Use the second slip until it is soiled and then remove it, and so on.

"Now, here is the trick to having clean slips later: When you stop in town overnight (or this can be done while the family is eating), go to one of the laundromats and leave your soiled clothes and pillowslips.

"There is nothing worse than returning home with a suitcase of soiled clothing! But, more important, doing this means you don't have to take so many pieces of underwear and nighties on long trips . . . which saves suitcase space."

COLD CANTEEN

From Massachusetts: "Here's a little tip for those taking short **trips** who hate to change drinking water.

"When we took such a vacation last year we filled a large plastic-type container with snap-on lid and placed it in the freezer a few days before departure.

"We put the bottle in the trunk of the car when we left, and as it thawed we had nice cold water all the time. It is amazing how long the ice lasted. Ours lasted for days."

Those little bottles that nasal spray comes in are handy for **traveling.** The suction cap with the spray hole can generally be lifted out and the bottle washed very carefully.

Fill this bottle with liquid soap and then replace the spray section and cap. These take very little room and are handy for washing nylons and such.

I have done the same thing with shampoo, but please make sure you tape the name of the new contents on the bottle in big letters so you will know what each bottle contains!

U

WASH DAINTIES IN PILLOWSLIP

From Michigan: "For those dainty **underthings** that people think must be washed by hand:

"The easiest and safest way I have found is to put them in a pillowcase, tie the end with a rubber band or string and put this sack of dainties in with the rest of the wash in which you use warm—not hot—water. I put mine in with the pastel colors that will not fade.

"This way the threads of the elastic will not get tangled in the other clothes. This saves lots of hand washing—and saves you lots of money, too.

"Sweaters are wonderful when washed this way. Just be sure that the pillowslip is not too full so that the clothes can get a good swishing around!"

INSTANT UPHOLSTERY JOB

From New Jersey: "Anyone who happens to have a small **vanity stool** (the kind with the round seat) can cover the seat with an ordinary shower cap! The elastic in the cap will hold it in place.

"If you want to change the color of the seat, buy an opaque colored shower cap. If you just want to protect the vanity seat, buy a clear plastic cap and stretch it over the top. This way the cushion is kept clean, yet the design and color of the fabric shows through.

"And for those who want to cover the whole stool, buy a shower cap and simply attach a ruffle under the elastic part. Just slip the cap over the seat. The ruffle may be made either six inches or floor length."

THE VELVET TOUCH

Here's a tip for those who use **velvet** ribbons or bows, etc.

When you prepare velvet ribbon for cutting, run a brushful of colorless nail polish across the ends. After it drys, take your scissors and cut through the "polished" part. You will have smooth edges that will never fray, ravel or curl up! Even red polish absorbs into black velvet and does not show the red color.

BEATING AN OLD BUGABOO—VENETIAN BLINDS

From a busy housewife: "To clean **Venetian blinds,** I close them first and *then* remove them from the window and take them out on the driveway or sidewalk.

"Lay them out full length and just turn the garden hose

on them! Turn them over and wash the other side the same
way.

"If you have soiled places . . . use a long-handled brush
with detergent and then rinse again.

"Stand the blinds up on their *sides* to drip (or hang over the
clothesline) for ten or fifteen minutes. I do not suggest that
you hang them longer than this. Do not *completely* dry them
until they are rehung. Replace the blinds on the window.
Fasten the bottoms by pulling them tight and they will dry
beautifully and *not shrink*."

From Arkansas: "When I wash my metal **Venetian
blinds,** I take a pair of my husband's old socks and put one
on each hand.

"I use one for the suds and one for wiping. This is a
wonderful way to keep from cutting up your hands."

And did you ever try inserting a small sponge in your right
hand *before* slipping on that sock?

This allows one to get a much better grip on the blind and
also holds the suds at the same time! Try it.

THERE'S THAT VINEGAR AGAIN!

And for all the mommies who are fortunate enough to
have little babies in diapers . . .

So many mothers complain that diapers are such a problem
to get soft and white! What follows tries to answer all of
your questions so that the diapers may be clean and soft again.

My method of washing diapers has been approved by doctors, institutes, etc., and even laundromats have written that
for the first time customers were getting beautiful results with
my diaper method.

It has been established by medical authorities that some
diaper rashes are caused by ammonia, an after-product of wet
diapers. This *can be neutralized* by rinsing your diapers in
vinegar water after washing them! There's my old friend
vinegar again . . .

Here's how:

After running your diapers through the complete washing
machine cycle . . . turn your machine on rinse *again,* fill
the machine only half-full of hot water and add one cup of
vinegar (color seems to make no difference). Then go through
the rinse and spin cycles and *do not rinse again!* Leave the

vinegar solution in the diapers. The vinegar odor will leave when the diapers are dried in a drier or on your clothesline.

I say . . . and will stand by it till my dyin' day . . . that, after proper washing, a rinsing in vinegar and water solution can't be beat.

Vinegar, in my estimation (and many manufacturers, chemists and laundry people have written that they agree with me), is about the best there is for rinsing. Take my word for it: Vinegar neutralizes the ammonia in diapers.

Tell you what. Take only half of your diapers and try this method on them for a few weeks and just feel and see the difference yourself between your present washing method and the Heloise method. Do your own testing . . .

Bet you will be mighty surprised!

Vinegar also helps to keep the rest of your laundry sweet and clean.

Do you have a favorite blouse or housedress that you wash and iron each week, and yet it never really smells fresh and clean? This problem is especially bad with navy blues and blacks.

This (in my short and understandable words . . . I hope!) is caused by perspiration which has accumulated and has not been neutralized enough by deodorants or by proper washing and rinsing. Wash the garment and rinse it well, then soak it in some strong vinegar water if all right for your material. *Then* take the garment in your hands and rub briskly. *Do not* rinse this vinegar solution out. Let dry and proceed as usual . . .

See what happens!

After a few times you will be quite pleased. You will be back to good, clean, sweet-smelling clothes again.

Many women have written that their ironing is easier after using the above method in their entire laundry on washdays.

So, if you have any of these problems, do try a vinegar rinse!

VINEGAR RINSE FOR SOCKS

From New Hampshire: "How can I remove the odor from soiled socks?"

After a thorough washing, rinse socks in one-fourth cup white **vinegar** to one gallon of water. Let 'em soak a while.

Squeeze during soaking. Do *not* rinse again (unless allergic to vinegar, but I have never met anyone who is!). Let dry in sunshine.

Most odors are caused from accumulated bacteria and soap film. This washing method will help get rid of the soap film and the bacteria will wash away.

Also makes for real black socks instead of those horrible gray "things" I see on some men.

From Montreal: "I take the crease out of a hem where a garment has been let down by pressing lightly, then using an eye dropper filled with white **vinegar** and running it across the crease, allowing some of the vinegar to run on the crease. Press with a warm (not hot) iron until it is dry. I can never tell where the hem has been let out."

A teen-ager writes: "I always add a little **vinegar** to the rinse water when washing wool skirts or sweaters . . . there will be no perspiration odor."

w

WAYS WITH WALLS

From Alaska: "Many people remove **wallpaper** by the usual hot-water method. The easiest way I know is to use a paint roller. Dip it in boiling water and wet the wallpaper.

"However, I found that the water dripped badly. I corrected this situation by adding some hot starch solution in my water. The thickness of the starch allowed the water to stay on the paper long enough to moisten it so that it can be easily removed. By using the paint roller or wallpaper paste brush it worked like magic.

"Using my pancake turner, and starting at the bottom of the wallpaper, I lift up the soaked paper and pull it up toward the ceiling and throw the rolls in the wastebasket."

A suggestion came from Iowa to remove **wallpaper** with equal parts of vinegar to equal parts of warm water—half-and-half. Simply dip a sponge in a solution and wet the paper through. Then take a scraper and go to work!

From Alabama: "When I removed the **wallpaper** from my bedroom, I discovered very uneven 'rough' plaster, no finish coat. The walls looked so bad they reminded me of road maps. I asked my hardware dealer what I could do at minimum cost.

"He recommended using texture paint to fill in the uneven places. There are inexpensive brands of texture paint and these can be tinted any shade you like. I used a dark shade to further hide the unevenness, and in some places applied it by rubbing it on with a rag instead of using a brush."

From North Carolina: "When white plaster **walls** have small holes made from hanging pictures and you don't have the time to order crack-filler, just put a white, powdered kitchen cleanser in a small bowl and mix it to a thick consistency with white shoe polish. Fill the hole with this mixture and smooth it on. When the mixture dries, the hole cannot be detected."

From Montana: "When hanging **wallpaper,** I place two pieces of toothpicks in a nail hole where a picture has been removed. When it comes time to replace the pictures, the nail holes are easily found!"

From Vermont: "I want to add an important note for those who want to know the tricks of patching **wallpaper.** My grandfather, who was a paperhanger, taught me this: When you're tearing your paper to patch, *always tear toward the wrong side of the paper.* It makes the patch almost invisible.

"This is especially wonderful if you have not been able to match your flowers quite well enough when hanging the paper. Just tear out a flower or other design to the wrong side of the paper and apply over the design *along the seams.* It will be hardly noticeable."

From Kansas: "Here is the way I remove grease spots from **wallpaper.** Naturally, the sooner you work with it the better.

"Just take a clean powderpuff and sprinkle the puff with white talcum powder and then rub the powderpuff over the spot. Repeat this process until the grease disappears.

"When the puff gets greasy, turn it over and use the other side. Be sure to keep dipping the puff in the talcum so it works into the grease. Let set a while and wipe off with a clean puff."

From Nevada: "This sounds silly but it works . . . stale, soft chunks of bread, rubbed over **wallpaper** in even vertical strokes, erase soil spots, even very visible fingerprints."

From a fresh-bread user: "For people who happen to get a dark stain from stove heat on their **wallpaper,** I would like them to know how I removed mine successfully. I used a piece of white, very fresh bread, and rubbed the mark. It vanished.

Fingermarks on wallpaper around the light switches are perfectly removed by an art gum eraser.

WHEN YOU CHANGE BRANDS

From Denver: "The man who installed our **washing machine** told me this:

"Every time you change to a different brand of soap or detergent, rinse out the machine with a water softener. The machine should go through the entire cycle, including the rinse.

"Otherwise a film or scum will be left on the clothes. Soap has a scum and detergent a film and these are left in the washing machine. You can't see it but it's there!"

TRY SALT-WATER TREATMENT

From Virginia: "Put a handful of salt in cold water and soak clothing in it for half an hour before **washing**. This will keep non-fast colors—especially red and black—from fading. The salt sets the color."

NO MORE TANGLES

From Connecticut: "Here's a little hint to pass along: Clothes with ties or sashes should be turned *inside out* before placing them in the **washing** machine. This will keep the ends from becoming tangled!"

SOCKEROO OF AN IDEA!

And a gentleman writes: "All those unmated socks with holes that our wives have in the house can be used . . . to jam paste **wax** in when you wax the car! When the sock gets dirty on one side, turn it over and continue waxing.

"Incidentally, I stole this idea from the woman who wrote in to your daily column and said this was the way she waxed her floors."

ROLL-ON WAX

From a busy housewife: "I have found the answer to **waxing** my floors! I bought a paint roller. The best type is one where I pour a liquid wax into the cavity. However, any type should do.

"I find that I never mark my floors in streaks as I used to (by pouring liquid wax in a spot and then trying to spread it), nor do I get too much in one spot and hit-and-miss in another corner. I feel that I save lots of liquid wax this way.

"One other thing about it: What I have left in the pan can be easily poured back into the bottle!

"My husband has attached my paint roller to an old broom handle. Now I don't even have to stoop!"

WEDDING WHITE

From New York: "What do you do about a **wedding gown** and veil after the wedding? When I pack it away, must it be cleaned, must it be professionally packed or can I do it myself?"

After much research, I finally went to the National Institute of Dry Cleaning and here is what we found out:

There is no known chemical treatment which satisfactorily preserves wedding gowns.

Dirt, light and moisture are the hazards. Light damages all fabrics, so keep your dress where there is no light.

Tissue is good to soften the folds of the dress and avoid creases which may become impossible to remove. White tissue is safest. Conceivably tissue color might transfer to the dress fabric . . . it's not likely, but it could happen if by some chance the package became damp.

Moisture is a serious hazard to cotton, silk, rayon and most fabrics—not as much so to dacron and nylon. So store your wedding gown in a dry place. High humidity can cause mildew, which can leave a ruinous stain. And keep the storage area dry.

Dirt is really the first villain to take care of. Be sure the dress is *completely clean* before you store it away.

Perspiration can cause stains and in time will weaken the fabric. If you have shields in your dress remove them before storing. Store them separately.

Food stains, champagne spots and so on are easiest to remove when they are fresh. They can become *impossible* to remove if they are allowed to set. They will attract moths, too. Even if the fabric is not one which a moth normally goes after, it will be damaged when the moths go for the food stains. Don't leave any starch in the fabric. Silverfish love starch.

Dry cleaners can take care of the whole problem. They will clean and professionally finish the dress, soften its folds with tissue and pack it in a special wedding box so constructed that no air will get in. Some boxes are windowed with clear plastic so that when you lift the lid you can show your grandchildren what you wore. But close the lid again so as not to expose the fabric to too much light. Store the box in a dark, dry place.

And may there be many pretty brides who later wear your wedding gown.

This is also a wonderful way to store and keep **"wedding white"** those little christening dresses, baptismal clothes, the baby's first pair of white booties. Don't forget to keep *those*, gals. Years later you will just love them with all your heart.

WATCH THOSE WINDOWS

When you are painting **windows,** try this plan to keep paint off the glass: Take newspapers or any paper with a straight edge, dampen well with warm water and spread them all over the windowpanes. They will cling there until you are finished with your job. When these are dry they are easily removed.

Instead of using newspapers or masking tape when painting **windows,** you can use a bar of softened soap! Paint will not stick to the glass this way and the soap is so easy to remove from the window. When paint dries, just wash the window with a sponge. If it's an outside job, you can wash the panes with a garden hose.

Paint spatters on **windows** can be removed easily with nail polish remover.

JACK FROST WAS HERE!

From Baltimore: "For those who live close to a neighbor and want to 'frost' a bathroom **window,** here is the method I have tried and found most satisfactory:

"I dissolve four tablespoons of epsom salts in one cup of beer and apply the mixture with a brush to the inside of my windowpanes. It is the best frosting I have ever seen.

"I apply the mixture with a two-inch-wide paintbrush. It not only covers the window, but looks like Jack Frost himself had been there! It dries beautifully, lasts a long time, and when washed off is easily reapplied. It's amazing how it crystallizes."

Try it, ladies! I tried the brush method and also the dabbing method. I found I got prettier Jack Frosts and crystallization by dipping a facial tissue (or a piece of terry cloth) in the mixture, and instead of wiping I just went dab, dab, dab. After you pour the crystals into a little bowl, put the beer in and stir a few minutes—all of the crystals will not dissolve—then just dab away. Real perky, I'd say. And the second day it's even more beautiful. More crystals, more opaque, and prettier. Water and a washrag removes it beautifully if you tire of it.

WINDSHIELD TRICKS

From Oregon: "In our car I keep ordinary baking soda in a large jar with a piece of soft cloth.

"When it rains, just dampen the cloth and put gobs of baking soda on it and wipe the automobile windows inside and out. The rain won't stay on the **windshield.** True magic!"

Did you know that nylon net is "the most" for washing bugs from automobile **windshields?**

Newspapers work beautifully for cleaning the **windshield** of a car. They clean perfectly and the papers can be thrown away.

". . . HAVE YOU ANY WOOL?"

One of the world's greatest tailors gave this advice for care of **woolen** clothing:

Iron it as *little* and as *seldom* as possible.

Hang on shaped hangers, or pad the hangers to conform to the shape of the shoulders.

In moist climates, hang the clothing overnight on the screened porch or where fresh air circulates. In dry climates, hang either in the laundry or the bathroom where there is steam in the air.

Touch up (with a steam iron) any parts that need special pressing. However, never iron a woolen garment quite dry; always leave the wool slightly damp and hang at once.

X-TRA, X-TRA, READ ALL ABOUT IT!

From Chicago: "I got tired of getting ragged and jagged fingernails from opening the little metal pouring spouts on salt boxes, detergent boxes, cereal, etc.

"I took a two-and-one-half-inch strip of cellophane tape, placed one end of it on the inside of the pouring spout and folded it back over, letting the other end of the tape stick to the outside of the metal tab.

"This serves as a plastic pull tab! Fingernails are no longer damaged from prying open the spouts."

A reader's answer to a weighty problem: "When a woman is trying to move a chest of drawers (and don't we all when we get bored), she should never attempt it while it is full. Remove all the drawers one by one and place them on the bed. The chest will then weigh less and slide easily. This also prevents marring floors!"

From an avid reader: "I have extra-long bottom sheets for our bed. So that they can be quickly recognized, I tip one corner with red nail polish. I never have time for any other markings. It takes months for the commercial laundries to wash it out!

"My most-copied idea: I use our freezer as a place for storing valuable papers. It is the one place in the house which is fireproof, and it can be locked if desired. I put the papers in tightly sealed plastic bags."

LEG ART

Sometimes when I am tired during the day, I sit on the edge of the bathtub and turn the faucets on. I let the water run over those tired feet and legs. Lush, relaxing, it makes you feel like a different person. Cleaning the tub won't be necessary. Just leave the drain open.

HAPPINESS IS A PLASTIC JUG

A reader who improvised: "The other night, I needed a hotwater bottle. Not having one available, I filled a gallon plastic bleach jug with hot water.

"I found it the best hot-water bottle I have ever used! Just lie on your side and curl up around it.

"It stayed hot for hours and hours. A towel can be wrapped around the outside."

TWO IDEAS FROM NEW ZEALAND

From a New Zealand housewife: "I keep my rolling pin wrapped in wax paper in my refrigerator. When it is thoroughly chilled, it is wonderful for rolling pastry in hot weather!

"A white fingernail pencil, such as the kind used for whitening underneath the nails, is excellent for touching up the discolored grouting between tiles in the bathroom. I just moisten it and mark!"

CRACKER-BARREL PHILOSOPHY

From a lover of crisp crackers: "Try storing them in the oven. If you have a pilot light, it will produce just enough heat to keep them crisp in damp weather.

"Also, once a big box of cereal is opened and gets soggy,

the contents can be made crisp again by putting them on a big cookie sheet and heating for a few minutes in the broiler or oven. Sure makes 'em good."

HOT LUNCH

From a working gal: "Here's my contribution for those who take lunches to work: Make use of the radiators while they are hot by wrapping a cheese sandwich in foil and placing it on the radiator. Turn it at least once during the morning . . . and by noon you will have a piping hot melted cheese sandwich!"

A BACHELOR SPEAKS

From California: "For heating canned foods such as pork and beans, spaghetti, tamales, peas, corn, beef stew, chili and so forth, I just cut the top off the cans and set the cans in a big pan of water (one-half the depth of the can) and cover it with a lid. Then turn the fire on.

"Presto! In no time at all, the food is hot, and I have no dirty pot to wash. Two, three, and even four cans can be warmed together in one big sauce pan. It saves this bachelor lots of energy."

BE PREPARED

From Virginia: "My husband works on different shifts.

"Since this entails his eating at one time and the rest of us eating at another, I solved the problem of having to prepare two different evening meals by saving my foil TV dinner plates from previous purchases.

"I prepare dinner for my husband at the appropriate hour. With what is left I simply make up six TV dinner plates for myself and the children. I dot my potatoes with butter instead of gravy, and put the extra gravy on the meat.

"Now, here's the good part:

"Since we eat the dinners the same evening there is no need to freeze them. We cover the TV plates with foil and put them in the refrigerator until ready to heat. When it is time for the rest of us to eat, I place the dinner in the oven and set it at 400 degrees for about fifteen or twenty minutes.

"When he is on the other shift I do it vice-versa.

"This is also an excellent idea for mothers who must leave children with a baby sitter. Dinners may be prepared in advance for the sitter and children with no extra effort on their part."

DOES EVERYTHING BUT THE DISHES . . .

From Texas: "Behold the lowly beer-can opener! And, in so doing, visualize the many uses I put it to in my kitchen, besides the one for which it was designed. I refer only to the slightly pointed end.

"As a shrimp deveiner, it does the job thoroughly with a minimum of effort and no breakage.

"As a potato peeler, it takes out the deep-set eyes quickly and efficiently.

"As a strawberry huller, the opener is the greatest!

"As a decorator of cucumbers . . . insert the point deep through a whole, unpeeled cucumber at one end and bring the opener firmly toward the other end of the cucumber. I

do this in rows about one-fourth of an inch apart. The result is attractive fluted rounds on the cucumber. When you slice it later, there is the tiny attractive touch of green when it is thinly sliced."

DID YOU EVER THINK OF . . . ?

From a reader: "Shelf paper has many good uses. It makes wonderful drawing paper for children.

"Colored shelf paper is good for wrapping gifts since it is strong and opaque as well as attractive. Bright-colored ribbon is attractive on white shelf paper when used for wrapping packages."

An answer to a sticky problem: "To remove masking tape and the gum it sometimes leaves on windows and glass, saturate a small cloth with fingernail-polish remover.

"If the tape won't come off easily, wet it thoroughly with the remover. This will loosen it. The remover will also remove any gum left.

"The gum will not remain on the windows if the tape is removed immediately after the paint becomes dry."

From a reader: "With all the soda pop we drink, I have learned to buy small rolls of foil and use a piece to wrap around the bottom of each bottle.

"Not only does this insulate the drink and keep it cold longer, but it also eliminates any water marks on tables."

A happy grandmother says: "I put corn plasters on the bottom of vases, fruit bowls, ash trays and figurines. This keeps the bric-a-brac from scratching surfaces. It really does the job!"

ODDS AND ENDS THAT WORK!

Save children's odd socks! If your child wears P.J.'s with footies attached and walks around the house before going to bed, just put some of these odd socks over the footies. Remove when the child goes to bed . . . nice clean footies! Stretch socks are even better than the regular kind.

Old towels may be used to make bath mittens for children. Cut the towel into the shape of a large mitten and stitch on machine or by hand. Children love them and even take a cleaner bath!

From a mother in Arizona: "I find the inside seams of infants' clothes (such as underpants) are often rough and irritating. Now I put my baby's things on him wrong side out! This way the rough seams do not bother baby and only the softness will touch his tender skin."

For children who cannot swallow a pill or tablet: place it in a teaspoon of applesauce and see how easily it will "go down!" (You'd be surprised at the number of grownups who cannot swallow a pill with a sip of water!)

TIMELY TIPS

From mother of four: "I bought a small plastic bucket at my dime store and attached a shower curtain ring to it. I hang this on the line and use it for my clothespins. It slides up and down the line beautifully.

"The new lightweight plastic utility pails are brightly colored and could be 'dolled-up' with some decals."

From an interested father: "If fathers would attach an extra handle near the bottom of each screen door, a small child could open the door himself. This would save many a door-opening for mother."

STORM SIGNALS

A woman from New Jersey offers this suggestion: "From about the age of three a child is afraid of lightning and thunder at night . . . so tell him that Mother Nature needs light to see where it is raining, and the thunder is excitement! Give a child a flashlight and he will love it. You can show him how he, too, can make a light go on and off easily and quickly!

"My child always falls asleep with a flashlight in his little hand during a storm. This is the only time he can play with a flashlight and I do believe that he enjoys a storm every so often!"

FEELING CLOTHESED IN?

From Boston: "Here is a tip I would like to pass on to other mothers. I fold my children's pajama bottoms inside of the tops when I put them away. I put the blouses or shirts inside of the jeans or shorts of the children's everyday playwear. This is a time-saver for both mother and children and keeps drawers from getting all messed up every time children reach for clothes in the morning and pajamas at night."

If anyone can come up with a solution as to how to get boys

(and girls, too) of all ages to pick up toys and clothes without nagging, bribing or beating, then I suggest that they be knighted!

One trick for boys of a certain sports-happy age is to get them to put dirty socks and such in a container made from a simulated basketball hoop. Sew a detachable bag for the "basket" and anchor it high on the wall. Great sport. Any time you have more than one boy in a room, something is going to be thrown! It might as well be a pair of socks tied together instead of a pillow.

Basketball hoops can be made with two wire coat hangers bent round, and the hooks bent to hang on a nail on the wall. The basket can be stitched from basketball net, matching drapery material or an old bed sheet. It hooks to the "hoop" with dime-store drapery hooks, detachable for easy emptying. The net string sacks that potatoes come in also make good baskets.

From a reader: "If you rip a hem at the office or school, or even at home, and just *have* to wear the garment—use cellophane tape to anchor the hem! Sure has saved me lots of embarrassment. And time."

DOWEL THE TOWELS

From a mother of small children: "If towel racks are not removable, and there are small children in the house . . . buy a home gripper kit.

"Put three grippers on each end of the towel, using the snaps on one end and the trip parts on the other. When these are fastened, you will have a roller that can easily be removed for washing. There will be no towels dropped on the floor by the kiddies."

TIP FROM SIR GALAHAD

From a bachelor in Arkansas: "For those who own cigarette lighters and can never find a flint, here's an idea that will save their nerves . . .

"Learn to keep the extra flints under the cotton inside the lighter.

"Not only will you never be without a flint, but you can

give yourself the title of 'Sir Galahad' and come to the rescue of somebody who needs one."

QUICK TRICKS

Ever buy a dress on which the belt had only "punched" little holes that tear easily—no metal eyes or stitching? Go around the edges of the holes on both sides of the belt with clear nail polish. Renew as needed.

To soften dried cream deodorant, drop a little water into the jar and close the top for a few hours. Presto! It's soft and usable again.

When the stoppers on perfume bottles are stuck, put the bottles in the refrigerator until thoroughly cold and then remove the stopper. If you twist the stopper back and forth when inserting it, it helps prevent later sticking of the stopper.

y

SMALL BUSYNESS

From Ohio: "As a grandmother with many grandchildren, I have found that there are wash-off crayons on the market. I highly recommend them to mothers who have **youngsters** in the home. They wash off any washable surface and out of children's clothes readily, and may be bought at any variety store."

From Massachusetts: "When my daughter was small, her friends who came to play would tell me they had to be home at a certain time. I always set the alarm clock and put it in the room where they were playing.

"The **youngsters** seemed to like not being told to leave when it was time to go home. And there was no danger of my getting busy and forgetting. Who can argue with an alarm clock?"

On bad days when your **youngsters** have to stay in the house and they're tired of all their toys and are "getting in your hair," try giving each of them a bar of soap and a dull knife. Any regular table knife is good for this. Mind you, I did not say the paring knife!

Place a newspaper on your kitchen table and let your child "carve." There is no telling what he will come out with, but you will at least keep him occupied and it will calm your nerves.

The soap will not be wasted. When he is through "messing," put the shavings in one of those old plastic bottles and add some water and let it soak. This soap can later be used for many things for Mother herself.

I find that bars of colored soap hold a child's interest. Baby soap is much softer and easier to carve and it does not break as easily. If you buy the large bar, you can break it into two pieces and have another piece for the next rainy day!

Here's another way to keep **young children** busy on those "bad" days: Save all your empty soap boxes.

The children love to stack them and make forts and houses with or without a card table. They build "highways" and drive their cars and bicycles through them. If the boxes fall, the children do not get hurt.

The boxes don't take up much room in a garage or basement, and when they get worn out . . . just throw them away. They may be replaced each week as another box is emptied when you do that inevitable laundry.

Rolls from paper towels and bathroom tissue, etc., can also be saved. They make nice, neat log cabins. Just fasten them together with paper clips.

RED — HOT

A mother writes: "If mothers with **young children** paint the tops of hot-water faucets with red . . . then teach the tots that 'red' means *HOT!* . . . it will keep many tiny tots from scalding their hands!

"Later, as the child grows and learns, the fingernail polish can easily be removed with polish remover."

WHEN THEY'RE FUSSY . . .

Here is a hint guaranteed not so much to save time as to spare the nerves of parents of **young children.**

For tots around two or three years of age who awaken night after night, cry loudly for a half-hour or longer and refuse to be comforted by a drink of water or any amount of love and rocking in a chair, try this:

Wash the child's face with some lukewarm water to awaken him. Once he is fully awake he can be comforted and quieted. I only wish I had known this when our daughter was going through this stage!

EASIER ZIPPING

Why not attach notebook rings to the **zipper** tabs on your children's boots and jackets?

The notebook ring makes it easier for a child to open and close a zipper.

When **zippers** stick on pillow or comforter covers, try running some bar soap over the zipper and it will work like magic!

Incidentally, if you do not use pillow covers, why not put your older pillowslips on the pillows before putting on the regular pair? This protects the pillow ticking and also makes the pillowslips look whiter, especially if the ticking is striped or colored!

Epilogue

Dear Friend:

Now that you have read this book, let me open your mind again to one thing you must never forget!

Don't work yourself to death!

Don't try to be a fanatical homemaker or let yourself become a house slave. That house will be there years after you are gone. Think about Martha Washington—*her* home must still be dusted every day! How about *that?*

Be yourself; do only what your energy allows for that one day.

If you don't want to do the laundry on Monday, who ever said you couldn't wash clothes at midnight on Wednesday if you happen to be in the mood? If it stacks up for two weeks, that's O.K. in my book as long as your family has clean clothes to wear from day to day. Doctors have written and asked me to tell you this. They all approve of taking advantage of that burst of energy when it hits. So use it.

If you are in the mood to let off steam—blast off, gals! Psychiatrists who have written say this is the greatest thing for a housewife. Let out those things that build up inside of you. At least those listening might know you mean business (and I'll bet it will bring results, too!).

Just keep your heads high, and remember that I love each of you with all my heart and soul.

Heloise

Index

Index

a

Accidents: emergency treatment of, 2-3; preventing, 1-3

Adhesive tape for baby's first shoes, 17

Alarm clocks: for calling Johnny home, 5; in playpen, 86; for small guests, 215; taking tick out of, 4-5; for timing medicine, 84

Aluminum pans: cleaning outside of, 5-6; cleaning with ammonia, 5

Ammonia: cleaning black crepe, 43; cleaning chandeliers, 42; cleaning pockets, 139; getting at mildew in grout, 123; removing brown from pans, 5-6

Amusing children; *See also* Toys and amusements

Apothecary jars for food storage, 69

Apron: "hair-do," 6; sewing, 7

Artificial flowers, cleaning, 67-68

Aspirin, danger to children from, 1

Automobile windshields: in rain, 205; washing and cleaning, 206

Automobiles: pennies for meter, 10; scratches in, 9-10; washing, 8-9; use of window shade in, 9

b

Baby: caring for rubber toys, 12; cleaning shoes, 170; fasteners for baby's bedding, 26; first shoes, 17; making gift blanket, 73; mattress cover for crib, 26; play-pen ideas, 85-86; preserving christening clothes, 204; rough seams on clothes, 211; sheets for bassinet, 26-27

Baby food jars for children's paint, 7

Baby oil for removing paint from skin, 138

Baby's bath: giving vitamins in, 12; making a pleasure of, 12; with mother, 13; plastic clothes basket for, 13

Baby's bottles: improvised warmer for, 18; washing crystal clear, 18

Baby's shoes: cleaning, 170; learning right from left, 17; preventing slipping, 17

Bacon: curl-free, 18; using flour in frying of, 18-19

Baking pans, greasing, 19

Baking soda for windshield, 205

Barbecue sauce, 178

Bassinet, sheets for, 26

Bath: baby and mother together, 13; cleaning rubber toys, 12; giving baby vitamins in,

AMERICA'S CHAMPION

Heloise

HOUSEKEEPER

- HINTS FOR WORKING WOMEN
- ALL AROUND THE HOUSE
- HOUSEKEEPING HINTS
- KITCHEN HINTS
- WORK & MONEY SAVERS

Hundreds of helpful hints for easier, speedier, money-saving ways to accomplish every household task.

▼ AT YOUR BOOKSTORE OR MAIL THE COUPON BELOW ▼